WITHDRAWN
From the
Dean B. Ellis Library
Arkansas State University

DEAN B. ELLIS LIBRARY

THE STRUGGLE FOR POWER

Volume 5, Sage Library of Social Research

SAGE LIBRARY OF SOCIAL RESEARCH

Also in this series:

1. **DAVID CAPLOVITZ**
   The Merchants of Harlem: A Study of Small Business in a Black Community

2. **JAMES N. ROSENAU**
   International Studies and the Social Sciences: Problems, Priorities and Prospects in the United States

3. **DOUGLAS E. ASHFORD**
   Ideology and Participation

4. **PATRICK J. McGOWAN and HOWARD B. SHAPIRO**
   The Comparative Study of Foreign Policy: A Survey of Scientific Findings

5. **GEORGE A. MALE**
   The Struggle for Power: Who Controls the Schools in England and the United States

6. **RAYMOND TANTER**
   Modelling and Managing International Conflicts: The Berlin Crises

7. **ANTHONY JAMES CATANESE**
   Planners and Local Politics: Impossible Dreams

8. **JAMES RUSSELL PRESCOTT**
   Economic Aspects of Public Housing

9. **F. PARKINSON**
   Latin America, the Cold War, and the World Powers, 1945-1973

The Struggle For Power

Who Controls the Schools in
England and the United States

George A. Male

Volume 5
SAGE LIBRARY OF
SOCIAL RESEARCH

 SAGE PUBLICATIONS   Beverly Hills   London

Copyright © 1974 by Sage Publications, Inc.

All rights reserved. No part of this book may be reproduced or utilized in any form of by any means, electronic or mechanical, including photocopying, recording, or by any information storage and retrieval system, without permission in writing from the publisher.

For information address:

SAGE PUBLICATIONS, INC.
275 South Beverly Drive
Beverly Hills, California 90212

SAGE PUBLICATIONS LTD
St George's House / 44 Hatton Garden
London EC1N 8ER

Printed in the United States of America

International Standard Book Number 0-8039-0327-8 (P)
0-8039-0328-6 (C)
Library of Congress Catalog Card No. 73-88907

FIRST PRINTING

*To my wife Shirley and
our daughters Ellen Gradick,
Barbara Isenhour and Jan Male*

TABLE OF CONTENTS

Chapter	Page
Preface	9
Acknowledgments	11
1. The Struggle for Power	15
2. Vast Powers of the National Government	25
3. Signs of Growing Centralized Control	39
4. Teacher Power	83
5. The Bosses—Erosion of Authority	109
6. The Death of Local Initiative	135
7. Grassroots Democracy	147
8. Conclusions	185
Index	197
About the Author	199

PREFACE

Both England and the United States are democracies where groups compete for a share of the decision-making power which determines the direction in which the society shall move. Schools are important in both countries, and who controls the schools is a matter of concern to a number of interested parties and agencies—including the national government, local governments, teachers and administrators, special interest groups, and ordinary citizens. This book traces the struggle for power to control the schools. The major emphasis is on England but frequent comparisons are made with the United States.

This book should be of interest to all persons concerned about such matters as the Black-white conflict over community-controlled education, teacher militancy, student protest, growing national government power at the expense of local initiative, and the effect of bureaucracy on individual freedom. It should be of value also to American educators and citizens who have become interested in the "open" or "free" schools of England, since the outcome of the struggle between freedom and heavy-handed authority may well depend on who controls the schools.

ACKNOWLEDGMENTS

Many persons over the years have helped me to understand England and its educational system. Notable among the English educators are Joseph Lauwerys and Brian Holmes of the Institute of Education, University of London. In the United States my doctoral advisor, Claude Eggertsen, brought me into contact with Lauwerys in the early 1950s during one of his first visits to this country. It was Eggertsen also who deepened my interest in pressure groups seeking to influence educational policy and encouraged me to study teachers' organizations and their pressure group activities.

The shortcomings of the study are mine alone and probably relate to the fact that I speak from a particular cultural perspective, namely the American.

I am particularly indebted to my wife Shirley, who offered constant encouragement and penetrating criticism, and to the secretary of the Comparative Education Center, Mrs. Helen Marsh, who labored long and hard in the typing of the manuscript.

THE STRUGGLE FOR POWER

Who Controls the Schools in
England and the United States

Chapter 1

THE STRUGGLE FOR POWER

In both England and the United States the growing bureaucratization of society threatens to reduce man to a cog in a machine he no longer controls. As old-fashioned neighborhoods, villages and cities decay, the typical response of the individual citizen is to try to maintain his level of participation in those matters where he conceivably might have some influence, especially in those institutions which shape his own future and that of his children. One of the few remaining areas where participation by the individual citizen is possible is that of schools. But in the United States and in England a growing aggressiveness on the part of the national government threatens to reduce the freedom of local citizens to control their schools and the educational fate of their children. At the same time, some of the powers of teachers and school administrators to control the educational process have been curtailed by these same national governments. In both countries the national government may unwittingly be encouraging the bureaucratization process which in turn increases man's subservience to systems beyond his control.

The assertiveness of the national government is encouraged by some persons and groups who seek to improve the quality of the educational process; these include persons who have faith in uniform standards applied to a wide geographic area. In some cases they are liberals who have long felt that in both countries the national government tends to be on the side of social change, while local governments are equated with stability, which translates preservation of the status quo— whether this be priviledged economic groups, dominant ethnic groups, or whatever.

Others see the enforcement of social justice as something which can be done only by the national government. So in the name of equal educational opportunity, English onlookers applaud as the national government forces county and city governments to build comprehensive secondary schools for children from all socio-economic groups, while the old separate academic secondary schools (grammar schools), attended mainly by the bright middle-class student, are closed or absorbed by the new schools. Similarly, in the United States these groups applaud the federal government's actions in promoting racial integration of schools—at least until it involves their child.

What we have operating, even with those liberals of a left-of-center persuasion, is a conflict between loyalty to an old tradition of local autonomy, which in turn is linked to individual freedom, and response to the pressures of a complex and rapidly changing world, which calls for a firm hand at the tiller—i.e., national control. In England the matter is viewed as a question of whether England can maintain its place in the front ranks of the leading world powers without placing more power in the hands of its national government.

Partly to reassure themselves people in both countries speak of local control as if it were a reality, whereas the signs—especially in England—indicate that it is a myth. Even

The Struggle for Power

the Labor Party in England, which has openly advocated national government ownership of certain industries and national government seizure of the private schools because they cater to the priviledged groups, continues to speak of local control with considerable reverence. On the other hand, the Conservative Party, which identifies with local autonomy in a way reminiscent of conservative political groups in the United States, has added to the powers of the national government when in office by repeated interventions in local educational matters.

The myth of local autonomy in education in the United States has acquired the status almost of a religion with the American people. Most Americans now live in metropolitan areas and know, only through their reading, about the one-room country school, run by a school board representing the local farmers. Many adult Americans, however, went to school in towns and small cities where there was an elected school board and where people spoke of their neighborhood schools with affection. There are still over 15,000 of these school districts in the United States where local citizens are elected to the school board. There are even attempts in the largest cities to break up the city, for the purpose of administering the schools, into two or three dozen districts, each with its own elected school board. Some of these attempts at decentralization have floundered on racial hostility as the teaching staff, largely white, feel they are losing control over the teaching process and their own professional autonomy to angry citizens—sometimes not too well educated and largely Black. Some Black leaders, on the other hand, see local control of schools as a major weapon to achieve control over their communities.

Decentralization of large American school districts may be doomed, along with the whole tradition of local autonomy, as pressures build for a more efficient educational enterprise and a more standardized product.

Certainly in England local autonomy is on its way out, and

a recent national commission's report (Maud Report) calling for a reorganization of the 145 local educational units (Local Education Authorities) into 93 larger, and presumably more efficient, units probably won't help. Journals and books in England uniformly report that localism will die unless something is done to stem the tide. At the same time, stereotypes persist that each school in England is free to decide what to teach, how to conduct its business, and that each classroom teacher has a major voice in deciding what and how he will teach. Legend has it that the teacher in England is king in his own classroom.

Another legend in England has it that a stable partnership exists in education with control shared by local governments, the national government, and the teachers and their organizations. Parents and citizens usually are not specified as members of the partnership, but angry outcries by citizen groups in the 1960s and 1970s may change all that. Certainly the new aggressive posture of the national government calls into question the stability of the partnership.

The national government in England is taking over in areas reserved by tradition to local governments. It is happening under both the Labor and Conservative parties, though the former is more openly in favor of this development. Teachers' unions seem to favor national intervention, too, thinking that it will help push their point of view. In practice it can work either way, but what is being pushed, somewhat unwittingly, is a more assertive role for the national government and a diminishing role for other members of the partnership. Surprisingly, a parallel trend is that of growing citizen protest over educational issues, but these groups also encourage the national government to intervene—hoping, of course, that the intervention will be on their side and against a recalcitrant headmaster or Local Education Authority (LEA).

Beginning in the 1960s the national government began to apply long-range planning to education to bring it into line with the national plan to strengthen the economy. This has led to increasing attempts to coordinate education with other social services. Inevitably the burden of coordinating, and of disciplining those parts of the enterprise which get out of line, falls to the national government.

As the power relationships alter, not unexpectedly entrenched groups resist change. More importantly, the changes are limited in their scope and effectiveness by a framework of traditions and value preferences which can be called the English way of doing things.

The English Way

The starting point is the striking homogeneity which exists among the approximately 46 million people in England. As one English scholar put it, there are no deep racial or religious divisions, no clear geographic separation (such as north versus south); instead there is a "base of common understanding" which produces a great stability in institutions.[1] The influx of what the English call "colored" people from Pakistan, the West Indies, and former African territories—and subsequent outbreaks of racial incidents—has altered the picture slightly, but the new groups are not involved to any serious extent in the struggle for power nor in the day to day negotiations which are so important a part of the educational scene.

Negotiation is part of the English way, and this encourages pressure group participation; refusing to bargain would force citizens at election time to make an all or nothing kind of choice. The negotiation process is aided by the spirit of local self-determination which has been strong and is now threatened.

In the spirit of negotiation, and in deference to localism, the Department of Education and Science, which is the branch of the national government which handles education, customarily circulates drafts of proposed changes in policy to interested groups before instituting a change. Thus, the main teachers' organization, the National Union of Teachers (NUT), is consulted regularly by the Department of Education and Science. At times, however, the national government flexes its muscles by not consulting the interested groups or by ignoring their views. This was the case in 1958 when the national government instituted a new system of channeling national funds to local governments and dropping the procedure of earmarking or reserving a fixed percentage of the money for use by schools. This was done over the vigorous opposition of NUT. In 1965 when the national government issued its notorious Circular No. 10/65, which in effect forced local governments to consider the establishment of comprehensive secondary schools, it did not even consult the teachers' organizations beforehand. (In 1970, with the Conservative Party in power, the national government recinded Circular No. 10/65.) In general, however, the tradition of negotiation is respected and makes it easier for teachers' organizations to exert pressure.[2]

Teachers' groups yearly engage in negotiations over the salary scale, which applies to all areas of the country and allows for no local determination of teacher salaries. Salaries are negotiated rather than being decided by a legislature or a parliament, or by the county government, or by an administrator in a particular school. In the past the bargaining occurred between the teachers' organizations and officials from an organization representing all the county governments in England, with the national government being a very quiet and unobtrusive bystander. All that changed in the 1960s as the national government demanded and gained a major role in the negotiation process.

In a sense the national government intervened in the salary area because it felt that unreasonable demands were being made. Reasonableness is part of the English approach, and for pressure groups to get a hearing their demands have to be moderate and their needs well documented. The system tends to discourage extremism, but in cases of serious disagreement an appeal to the public is made by one or more of the contending groups via a nationwide campaign.[3] Such campaigns can involve publicity, demonstrations, and, in the case of the teachers' organizations, threats to strike and then actual strikes. Much of this activity is designed to encourage citizens to pressure the national government to intervene and inevitably adds to the trend of growing national power. Teachers' organizations, citizen groups and local governments all end up asking the national government to take action. As a result, the power relationships are changing in England.

The American Way

Things are changing in the United States also. The local school district used to be able to control its own affairs subject only to state laws, which allowed considerable latitude. Now the only choice left to many school boards is whether or not to participate in programs designed by the federal government, or by wealthy private foundations. The lure of outside money makes the matter of participation a foregone conclusion, especially as angry, tax-burdened citizens in district after district refuse to approve local school bond issues to support programs designed by the local school board and the superintendent of schools.

The little choice that was left to local school boards has disappeared in an increasing number of school districts which, by state law, must now negotiate with the teachers' organization about salaries, working conditions, and the like.

There is a growing awareness that schools in the United States are no longer able to remain aloof from pressure group politics, if indeed they were ever free to do so. In political struggles educators form pressure groups—partly to protect themselves from other pressure groups who would like to control the schools, and partly to compete with other groups of teachers for the available tax funds (public school versus private, higher education versus elementary-secondary, state colleges versus the university, and so on). As educators fight for funds they are engaging in politics in the best sense of the word, and they are indeed articulating priorities for the society.[4]

Politics in education is reflected in those school board elections where ethnic, racial, or religious groups are catered to. In New York City there must be an Italian on the school board, a Jew, an Irish Catholic, and so on. In Boston, Catholics tend to dominate the school board, and in Utah it is the Mormons. Similarly, in appointing assistant superintendents and principals in New York City there tend to be a certain number who are Catholic, Jewish, and so on. The failure of Negroes to get their share of these policy-making positions is one factor behind the attempts of Black citizen groups to capture control of their schools from the white, ethnic-dominated school board and the largely white teaching staff.

Peter Drucker and others have reminded us that our society is becoming education centered, and that educational expenditures in time of peace are likely to exceed any other type of expenditure. The structure, content and values undergirding American education are a matter of increasing political concern to more and more people. As Drucker put it, "Education is bound to become the focus of political life and political conflicts."[5]

The federal government no longer can remain aloof from struggle for control of education. Where racial factors are involved the federal government has intervened in a decisive manner. Recently, however, the liberals have become critical of impersonal bureaucrats in Washington and less enthused about federal government attempts to equalize. Many of the educational programs to help the poor, such as Title I of the Elementary-Secondary Education Act of 1965, are seen as failures. Yet more central control is seen by many liberals in the United States as necessary if we are to solve the ills of our society. This view is typified by the following comment:

> It is a curious thing, but true that as national rather than local influences become more pervasive in American education it becomes rather more generous spirited, just as large corporations tend to be less malicious than small shopkeepers.[6]

Other Americans continue to believe in local control in spite of the new emphasis on planning, efficiency and professionalization.

> Professional educators, politicians, or planners who operate from some center of power in education are not necessarily wiser, better, or more humane than amateurs, laymen, and local boards. A study of the mistakes inspired in the recent past by central educational authorities in other countries might be a salutary exercise for Americans who regard local control as one of the big remaining obstacles to reform.[7]

The recent tendency of the federal government to assert itself has aroused some concern. Yet, the federal government in the United States has a long way to go before it acquires the power over schools which the national government in England has.

NOTES

1. George Baron, *Society, Schools and Progress in England.* London: Pergamon, 1965, p. 1.
2. Ronald A. Manzer, *Teachers and Politics in England and Wales.* Toronto, Can.: Univ. of Toronto Press, 1970, p. X.
3. Ibid., p. 3.
4. For an analysis of teachers and politics see Nicholas A. Masters, "The Politics of Public Education," pp. 174-182 in Emanuel Hurwitz and Robert Maidment, eds., *Criticism, Conflict and Change: Readings in American Education.* New York: Dodd, Mead and Co., 1970.

5. As quoted in LuVern L. Cunningham, "Federal Intervention in Education," p. 183 in Hurwitz and Maidment, op. cit. Drucker has written extensively on the growing importance of education; see, for example, *The Age of Discontinuity: Guidelines to Our Changing Society.* New York: Harper and Row, 1969, pp. 311-348.

6. Edgar Z. Friedenberg, "Status and Role Identity in Education," p. 167 in C. A. Bowers, Ian Housego, and Doris Dyke, eds., *Education and Social Policy: Local Control of Education.* New York: Random House, 1970.

7. James D. Koerner, *Reform in Education: England and the United States.* New York: Delacorte, 1968, p. 49.

Chapter 2

VAST POWERS OF THE NATIONAL GOVERNMENT

In England the national government plays an important role in education. Many of the important regulations and rules for schools are laid down either by national laws passed by Parliament or by decrees and directives from the Department of Education and Science, which is part of the executive branch of the government.

The situation is much different in the United States where schools are governed very little by federal legislation or directives, and only slightly more so by legislation and directives from the state government. Each local community determines the essential character of its educational system and provides the major share of the money to finance its schools. There are a few important exceptions where federal legislation has been important; such as the act of 1862 leading to the establishment of the land-grant colleges, the Smith-Hughes Act of 1917 to stimulate vocational education, the National Defense Education Act of 1958 to encourage the study of science and foreign languages, and legislation in the 1960s to aid handicapped children and to improve the education of slum children. In none of these instances, however, did the national government issue an order to the local school districts. Instead, money was offered for specific areas of education which local governments could accept or reject.

In England the national government's Department of Education and Science does not operate schools or colleges, and it does not employ, pay, or dismiss teachers, or control the books used in school. National salary scales for teachers, however, apply to all regions of the country and are established by a national committee composed of representatives of the teachers' organizations on the employees' side of the table and representatives of the national government and local governments on the management side of the table. In addition, the national government usually announces a top figure which the total expenditures for teachers' salaries cannot exceed. Teachers' organizations are barred by law from negotiating salaries with local governments. Local governments, in turn, are barred from offering teachers more money than a neighboring community. Nationwide salary scales insure that counties and cities lacking in financial resources will not lose out in securing good teachers because another community can pay their teachers more, as happens in the United States when wealthy suburban school districts drain off the best teachers leaving rural areas with the leftovers. On the other hand, England's system penalizes an energetic community which has set higher standards for its children than the national government requires and wishes to expend additional money on education to achieve these goals. The danger is that local initiative which is not allowed to function will dry up and a tradition of inaction and apathy will develop.

The powers of the national government in England to control schools are vast, thanks to the Education Act of 1944, but for a long time no Minister of Education (the title was changed in the 1960s to Secretary of the Department of Education and Science) dared exercise his powers to the fullest. It was widely held that for him to do so would generate a government crisis. By the mid 1960s it was becoming clear that many of the powers were beginning to be used, and warnings were sounded by scholars.

> We have by the 1944 Act given the Minister, and through him the Ministry, immense powers; and although so far they have been used temperately that does not diminish the need for vigilance to ensure the continuance of local and individual freedoms. There have already been two or three serious clashes between the centre [national government] and the circumference, and there no doubt may be many others before we have forged an accepted tradition about the frontiers of direction and control in the administration of the 1944 Act.[1]

It is now the national government that decides the standards for school buildings, including the size of teaching areas, playing fields, and cost per square feet. Most important of all, the national government decides whether a school proposed by the local government will be included in next year's building plans. Thus, the national government not only tells local governments how they will spend funds supplied by the national government but also sets limits on how local funds can be used.

The powers of the national government extend down to such details as to whether the teacher will be burdened with the task of supervising lunch periods. In the 1950s, and again in the 1960s, teachers' organizations and local governments reached an impasse in regard to assignment of teachers to lunch period duty, and the national government stepped in to conduct the negotiations to resolve the conflict. Moreover, the teachers' organizations encouraged this intervention.

Some of the powers of the national government are negative, as for example when it tells local governments that they cannot build a new school. At times the national government has refused permission not because the need for another school was disputed but because the national government did not approve of the type of school proposed.[2] Churches are also told that they cannot open a school since church schools (called voluntary schools) in England receive public funds in return for submitting to government control. Public schools (called county schools) are required by a national law to teach a course in religion, and the syllabus for the course must be approved by the national government. If the national government disapproves of the syllabus submitted by a particular county it can appoint a committee of experts to draw up a new one. In addition, the national government has a staff of inspectors (HMI's—Her Majesty's Inspectors) who have the right to inspect the courses in religion.

The national government also has a veto power over selection of the head administrator for the county and large city school systems. In the United States he would be called superintendent of schools; in England he is called either chief education officer or director of education. The list of candidates for the position of chief education officer must be submitted to the national government, which can strike names from the list. The local government is then free to choose from those remaining on the list.

Even the pay of university professors is determined by the national government. The universities in England describe themselves as autonomous, but the governing board of each university has no control over the salary scale. The scale is set by the Department of Education and Science, often after receiving secret advice from the independent University Grants Committee, made up of high ranking administrators and professors appointed by the national government.

As the national government got deeper into national planning in the 1960s, it began to talk about bringing the salaries of university professors into line with other occupations. Such talk frightened the Association of University Teachers, to which many professors belong, and the Association has begun to agitate for the establishment of formal machinery whereby university professors, through their organization, could negotiate their salary scale with the national government. It is worth noting that the professors did not suggest something like the American model where each institution of higher education sets its own salary scale or procedures for determining salary.

The universities in England acknowledged the right of the national government to regulate them as early as 1946 in a statement prepared by a committee representing the heads of the universities (usually called vice chancellors):

> The Universities entirely accept the view that the Government has not only the right but the duty to satisfy itself that every field of study which in the national interest ought to be cultivated in Great Britain is in fact being adequately cultivated in the University system, and that the resources which are placed at the disposal of the Universities are being used with full regard both to efficiency and to economy.[3]

The teachers' colleges (now called colleges of education) theoretically are run by county governments and by churches, but since 1944 the national government has kept tight control over salary levels, staffing ratios, expansion, and the basic design of the training program. When it came time in the late 1950s to raise the length of the program from two to three years, it was the national government that made the decision. It is true that various educational groups had advocated the change from 1919 onward, but in England individual colleges of education could not institute such a change; nor could the local governments which own the colleges make such a change—that power resides with the national government.

In vocational and technical education, where the equipment and materials are expensive, decisions have to be made as to which institutions will offer which programs. Such decisions at the post-secondary level are made by the national government though the schools are owned by city and county governments. Any new course, or new curriculum, must be approved by the Department of Education, and Science, which usually takes the advice of the national school inspectors (HMIs). Thus, a technical college run by a Local Education Authority (LEA) is not free to develop a new program, for example in computer sciences, without getting approval from the national level. Whether this inhibits imaginative designing of new and needed programs is worth considering. Vocational and technical courses at the secondary school level do not require approval from the national level, but "suggestions" from the Department of Education and Science are usually heeded.[4]

One obvious source of national government influence stems from the fact that it supplies 60 percent of the funds for schools, and local governments provide only 40 percent. (In the case of the universities, 80 percent comes from the national government.) There are, of course, more centralized countries, such as France, where 85 percent of the funds for elementary and secondary schools come from the national government. In the United States the figure fluctuated between 4 and 8 percent in the 1960s, with approximately 55 percent of school funds coming from local governments and 40 percent from state governments.

It has been suggested that the decisive factor behind the educational reforms of the 1955-1965 period was the growth in gross national product (GNP) and the rising percentage of GNP devoted to education.[5] In England it is primarily the national government that decides how much of the GNP will go for education.

The national government's power in fiscal matters can also operate in a negative way. This was illustrated in 1969 when it announced a 3-1/2 percent limit for local governments on increases in educational expenditures over the previous year. For some LEAs this meant the delay or elimination of new programs and cutbacks in old programs. In Warwickshire this meant that the swimming program in elementary schools was eliminated, money for books was cut, and the number of teachers for special education classes was cut by eleven. Similarly Kent adult education classes tripled the fees charged participating adults. Local governments in the United States also set limits on educational expenditures, but this is a national government prerogative in England when it chooses to overrule LEAs.

The assertion of national powers is more understandable as we get beyond the myth of local control and see the powers which reside with the national government, and have resided there for a long time. There is a tradition of national government intervention which goes back to the mid-nineteenth century in contrast to the local control tradition of the United States.

The strength of the American tradition is related to the fact that public schools in the United States were, and are, the creation of interested people in individual communities all across America. In England, on the other hand, most of the schools came into being through the efforts of wealthy benefactors centuries ago, or through the work of church societies and the stimulus of national laws—more particularly the laws of 1870, 1902, and 1944. Two English educators[6] have dramatized the difference by placing the following description of the founding of American schools alongside a description of the origin of England's schools, written by an Englishman:

> That system [of public schools in the United States] was not imposed from above by a strong central government or an influential intellectual class. Rather were its foundations laid by relatively untutored farmers who established one-room district schools in rural neighborhoods as they moved across the continent.[7]
>
> ... the mass of the English people have never yet evolved genuine schools of their own. Schools have always been provided for them from above in a form and with a content of studies that suited the ruling interests.[8]

It is important to note that the first public funds for schools in England came from the national government rather than from local government. Moreover, the schools receiving the funds were not community-run but instead established and controlled by national church societies. This is in contrast to the United States tradition of local communities taxing themselves to support their community-controlled schools.

In England in the first part of the nineteenth century, the national government was very reluctant to support schools with funds. The church societies, called voluntary societies, built such schools as there were.

> The support of the State for this effort was feeble, partly because direct Government activity of all kinds was contrary to the English conception of politics, and partly because the voluntary bodies would not allow to the State that measure of control without which the vote of large sums of public money could hardly be expected.[9]

In 1833 the National Government initiated annual grants to the church schools and soon after, through its Committee of the Privy Council, began to set conditions which the schools had to meet in order to receive the grants. The early government regulations were relatively mild but not so the "Revised Code," issued in 1861, which drastically affected the curriculum and teaching methods in a manner which the teaching profession later came to denounce as bad educational practice.

In the 1860s the private secondary schools were investigated and regulated by acts of Parliament. Even the universities did not escape. Parliament passed acts in the 1850s which regulated the universities, and the Act of 1871 forced both Oxford and Cambridge to cease being "church colleges" for Anglicans alone, and made them open to members of other faiths as well.

The English tend to take a positive attitude toward these

early encroachments of the national government. As the English see it, these laws tended to relieve the universities and the private schools of restrictions growing out of ancient rules set by wills, endowments, and earlier governments. Thus, after the nineteenth century acts of Parliament, new subjects and new types of students could be admitted, and the faculty could be drawn from a broader cross section of society.

Early in the twentieth century the national government, through the Act of 1902, ordered local governments to give local tax money to church schools. Soon after, the national government stepped in to regulate schools directly with the Regulations for Secondary Schools issued in 1904 by the national government through its Ministry of Education, which at the time was called the Board of Education. Nothing like these direct and detailed regulations for schools have ever been issued by the federal government in the United States, except in the 1960s and 70s when the federal government issued specific directions with regard to integration of white and Negro students and faculty. Even here the executive branch of the government, via the Department of Health, Education and Welfare, has abandoned most of this activity and left it to the federal courts. This withdrawal was done partly because of the political furor which this federal activity engendered and partly because the federal government does not have, and never has had, a corps of federal agents to supervise local schools in the way in which England's HMIs do.

The HMIs, according to a former chief inspector, in a sense represent an affront to the teaching profession. [10] The inspectors, representing the interests of the public, act as watchdogs over schools and teachers. In the beginning of such inspection, in 1839, teachers were badly prepared, often incompetent, and certainly could not claim to be professionals.

Interestingly enough, the United States did not feel the need for such inspectors, perhaps because school administrators in the local system tended to assume the supervisory role early or because the local school district system with small areas and elected school boards has meant, in effect, that all citizens watch over the schools. In practice, however, less than 50 percent of the eligible voters cast their ballots in a typical school board election in the United States.

Originally the English inspectors checked only on the schools set up for the poor, and the emphasis was on inspection of the religion classes. For the first few decades the inspectors tended to be clergymen.

As schools, and England in general, became more secular, especially with the rise after 1870 of public schools not affiliated with a church, the inspectors increasingly were lay people, usually "gentlemen." Until the first decade of the twentieth century the school inspector typically was a graduate of Oxford and Cambridge, and often had no teaching experience. NUT, the teachers' association, protested repeatedly, and eventually won the national government over to a policy of promoting outstanding elementary-school teachers to fill some of the vacancies in the inspectorate.

The HMIs are employees of the Department of Education and Science, though popular mythology would have it that they constitute an autonomous corps responsible to the Crown. The inspectors do have a measure of independence and do not push an official point of view, though they are not expected to flaunt important national government directives (such as the circular of 1965 pushing LEAs to establish comprehensive secondary schools).

The role of the inspector tends to be that of an interpreter of national policy to the local governments and in turn informing the Department of Education and Science of the views and problems of the LEAs. In addition, they spread word of innovations in curriculum and method via the 100 or so short courses (ten days or less) which they offer to interested teachers each year. Formal inspection of a particular school occurs very infrequently; once every five years is the goal, and even that often proves unmanageable for lack of staff.

What is the effect of the system of HMIs in terms of extending the control of the national government? Some Americans interested in imposing national standards on American school districts see the English HMIs as enforcing high academic standards and avoiding narrow localism.[11] An English educator, Edmund King, speaks of the inspectorate as a "rather polite advisory service" which actually works.[12] He describes the central control thus exercised as "powerful though gentlemanly." The disadvantages are summed up in the term "hesitation." Things move, if they move at all, in a jerky fashion; there is little of the streamlined efficiency which the English see as being much sought after in America.

The largest teachers' organization in England, the National Union of Teachers, asserted before a select committee of Parliament in 1968 that the existence of the corps of HMIs prevented the national government from controlling the curriculum area.[13] Presumably there is no need to issue official curricula when your agents are out in the field effectively spreading the word.

The English have another means of controlling the curriculum, namely the nine regional examination boards which test students at the end of what Americans would call the tenth and twelfth grades to determine who is doing well in school. In effect the examinations determine who will be admitted to the universities, and secondary schools are constrained to offer what the examinations require.

The examining boards developed originally to test private school students hoping to enter the universities, but in 1917 the national government, via the Board of Education (which later became the Ministry of Education), placed all these boards under the supervision and control of a new Secondary School Examinations Council,[14] which in typical English fashion was declared to be "autonomous." From these early beginnings have evolved the present nine examining boards which are called autonomous but regularly submit their examinations to the national government (Department of Education and Science) for acceptance. Hence, there is voluntary acceptance of "guidance" from the national government, and the examinations of the nine examining boards tend to be similar.

Guidance from the national government is on the increase, and the decade of the 1960s and the early years of 1970s provide evidence of a shift in power with regard to who controls the schools.

NOTES

1. W. O. Lester Smith, *Education in Great Britain*, fourth ed. London: Oxford Univ. Press, 1964, p. 175.

2. Richard Batley, Oswald O'Brien, and Henry Parris, *Going Comprehensive: Educational Policy-Making in Two County Boroughs*. London: Routledge and Kegan Paul, 1970, p. 8.

3. Committee of Vice-Chancellors and Principals, *A Note On University Policy and Finance in the Decennium 1947-56*. Privately printed, 1946, p. 14, as cited in Harold C. Dent, *Universities in Transition*. London: Cohen and West, 1961, p. 79.

4. Interview with high-ranking official in the Department of Education and Science. Times Educational Supplement (London), May 23, 1969, p. 1708.

5. A. D. C. Peterson, "Educational Reform in England and Wales, 1955-1966." Comparative Education Review, Vol. XI, No. 3, Oct. 1967, p. 289.

6. George Baron and Asher Tropp, "Teachers in England and America," p. 546 in A. E. Halsey, Jean Floud and C. Arnold Anderson, eds., *Education, Economy, and Society*. New York: Free Press, 1961.

7. George S. Counts, *Education and American Civilization*. New York: Teachers College, Columbia Univ., 1952, p. 454.

8. Sir Fred Clark, *Education and Social Change*. London: Sheldon, 1940, p. 30.

9. A. D. C. Peterson, *A Hundred Years of Education*, second ed. London: Gerald Duckworth, 1960, p. 11.

10. John Blackie, *Inspecting and the Inspectorate*. London: Routledge and Kegan Paul, 1970, p. 1.

11. H. G. Rickover, *American Education: A National Failure.* New York: E. P. Dutton, 1963, p. 283.
12. Edmund J. King, *Other Schools and Ours,* third ed. New York: Holt, Rinehart and Winston, 1967, p. 111.
13. Blackie, op. cit., p. 60.
14. George Baron, *Society, Schools and Progress in England.* London: Pergamon, 1965, p. 114.

Chapter 3

SIGNS OF GROWING CENTRALIZED CONTROL

The noticeable shift in power among the members of the partnership governing education in England came with the 1944 Education Act.

To insure that the Local Education Authorities (LEAs) would implement the 1944 Act fully, the national government was given far-reaching powers to control education. The old Board of Education now became the Ministry of Education with a mandate to develop a national policy of education. Each of the LEAs was to formulate a comprehensive plan for elementary and secondary schooling in its region and submit the plan for approval to the Ministry of Education. In addition, each LEA had to formulate plans for the development of vocational education, or further education as it is called in England, and submit these to the Ministry.

The shift of power to the national government was done openly and deliberately.

The bestowal of almost absolute sovereignty over education upon the Minister [of Education] was made deliberately by Parliament, and was not, as some like to suggest, a slice of new despotism unobtrusively slipped into the bag from under the counter. Mr. Butler was in fact applauded when he declared that it was intended that the Minister should "lead boldly and not follow timidly." Parliament of its own initiative went even further than he asked by inserting Section 68 into the Act, giving the Minister power to prevent local education authorities, governors, or managers from acting unreasonably.[1]

Greater control by the national government was also extended over church schools in return for greater support from public tax money. The church schools had a choice of accepting a status with less government control and less government aid or one of more aid and more control. Those church schools accepting the larger amount of government aid were called "controlled" schools while the others were "aided" schools. In the "controlled" schools teachers were to be appointed by the local government (LEA), which was also to be represented on the board of governors of each church school. Moreover, these "controlled" church schools could only offer sectarian religious classes two days per week.

The Act of 1944 also gave the national government power to inspect private schools not receiving public funds and to close "inefficient or inadequately equipped schools."

By the 1960s the powers of the national government were in full view. Scholars were beginning to sound a warning and at the same time trying to explain why growing centralization had occurred. Part of the answer lay with that section of the 1944 Act which gave public money to church schools in return for a measure of government supervision. Of necessity the national government had to formulate a set of guidelines which were clear and firm. As schools, both church and county, have turned to the national government for increasing amounts of money and for other forms of aid, the

Signs of Growing Centralized Control

directives have multiplied. Those Americans in the 1970s who urge that the federal government's share of school financing be increased from the present 4 percent to 30 percent might well anticipate a similar growth of federal directives.

The growing centralization in England may be related to the fact that the long-time swing from the individualism of nineteenth century England to collectivism is just about complete, and there is far less objection to national government initiative in social legislation.[2] The slowness of needed social change under the system of local control may have hastened the shift to national control.

> The only major country of western Europe to survive until 1944 without a Ministry of Education, England now seems to be moving towards a greater measure of central control. The climate of opinion about this slow centralization is less hostile than ever before. There are many reasons for this, among them the uncertainty as to where responsibility lies, the desire to equalize educational opportunities everywhere, the slowness of the present mechanisms of change, the comparative indifference of local electorates as compared with the passion that educational matters are beginning to arouse at the national level, and, above all, the determination of the central government to see that "he who pays the piper, calls the tune."[3]

The delay for a number of years in using the powers granted to the national government by the 1944 Education Act has been explained as follows: a) for some time there was little disagreement over the educational job to be done; b) it took a while for the idealism left over from the war to dissipate; and c) prominent officials at local and national levels had much in common and worked well together. All this began to change in the late 1950s as 1) new men took over leadership positions in the Ministry of Education and wondered why the powers were not being used; 2) disagreements over key educational problems developed among educators; and 3) the expansion of education raised the issue of priorities and the need to use resources efficiently.[4]

Modern technology exerts a demand for efficiency and England's prospects for the future are increasingly linked to the development of technology, especially now that the colonies are gone and England must compete for world trade on its own.[5] Moreover, "the pace of change is so fast everywhere that some coordination or phasing of development is accepted as a critical responsibility of statecraft in all countries."[6]

Additional pressures for centralization grow out of the need for innovation and reform in education, and the widespread feeling that this will occur only with greater national leadership. It is fairly common for English educators to assert that "since 1944 innovation in education has increasingly tended to be initiated from the centre."[7] It isn't that the national government originates these ideas in every case but rather that it is willing to pick up good ideas from whatever source and disseminate them, and even push hard for them. Examples of such national government initiative include the movement to make comprehensive schools universal and the establishment of first-rate colleges of technology (CATs), and then their conversion into technical universities. The example of the CATs contrasts sharply with the rise of urban universities (Leeds, Sheffield, and so on) near the end of the nineteenth century through the initiative of interested individuals and city governments. Further examples of recent initiative from the national government include the extension of the teacher training program to three years and then to four years, with a degree offered to selected individuals. In some cases the national government had to pressure some of the universities to accept the new degree (B.Ed.) for teachers.[8]

In the 1960s the Department of Education and Science became a more important and powerful force as education became a more important element in national policy, and as the Department was given supervision over higher education, research councils, the arts, and sports.[9]

Even earlier, however, there were signs that the national government was extending its powers. In the late 1950s the shortage of teachers in some regions of England caused the national government, via its Ministry of Education, to issue a directive setting quotas on how many teachers each Local Education Authority could hire. The quotas remained in force throughout the 1960s and were supported as necessary by NUT, the largest of the teachers' organizations. In the 1970s, however, as a surplus of teachers materialized in England, as it did in the United States, NUT began to speak of the need to find jobs for all teachers and to use the surplus to good advantage, for example cutting down the size of classes. In April 1972, the Department of Education and Science announced that the quotas were now to be regarded as a minimum and not a maximum and LEAs were encouraged to hire beyond the quota. The national government, in effect, raised the quota and demonstrated again where the control of teacher supply lay. No LEA could really hire additional teachers without extra funds, and 60 percent of school funds come from the national government. Moreover, almost all supplemental grants to handle emergency situations come from the national government.

In 1938 the cost of education was shared almost equally between local governments and the national government. By 1953 the Government's share had risen to 60 percent, and in the 1960s several different groups suggested that it be increased further.

At the annual conference of the Conservative Party in October 1962 several resolutions called for a reduction of the burden on local governments by having the national government assume a larger share. Around the same time some of the LEAs began to express favor for such action, and members of Parliament from both major parties suggested that the

Minister of Education consider whether the ratio of 60 percent national support and 40 percent local might not be changed. Other groups joined the clamor, including the National Union of Conservative and Unionist Associations and the National Federation of Parent Teachers Associations.

In 1962 the president of the group representing the education committees within the Local Education Authorities (the Association of Education Committees) called for more initiative from the Minister of Education. In analyzing his speech, the *Times Educational Supplement* (London) endorsed the new line of reasoning that there was nothing to fear from growing central power.

> It is not only in the field of salaries that the Minister is now making his presence felt; Ministry research and projects such as the curriculum study group are giving the Centre a position of authority which local education committees cannot challenge.... There is no reason for local authorities to regret this trend. A strong centre does not connote dictatorship. It does not mean that a uniform pattern will be imposed on all the diverse parts of England and Wales.[10]

At the same time the *Times Educational Supplement* criticized the national government for not using its powers fully.

> It often appears that the Minister shelters behind the division of powers, on the grounds that such and such an action would not be possible because it is the province of the local authorities. The indications are that he need no longer feel himself so restricted, and that, with the cooperation of the local authorities, he is in a position to play an active leading role.[11]

The economists joined in the clamor for more central leadership, including John Vaizey of the Labor Party who wrote extensively on education and control. Vaizey advocated more centralization in the financing of schools, but he also urged more central control since there must be a national policy on many educational matters. At the same time he warned that a too powerful Ministry of Education could be dangerous because of "the dim conventionality of so many modern civil servants."[12]

Financing of Schools

Demands for the national government to carry a heavier proportion of the cost of education continued, but as the national government began to provide aggressive leadership, objections arose from a variety of sources, including the *Times Educational Supplement,* which earlier had been in favor of such leadership, NUT, and leading spokesmen for the Conservative Party.

The *Times Educational Supplement* saw a clear link between national financing of schools and national control.

> ... up to now we have always supposed that educational progress and the efficiency of the system depend on a vital element of local control. Do we want to abandon this? If all the money comes from the centre we can be sure that all the control will come from there, too.[13]

The head of NUT, in 1965, suggested that the liberty of the classroom teacher was dependent on the maintenance of a fine balance between local and national control. He hoped that the national government would increase its grants for education without upsetting the balance of power.[14]

By 1965 there was a growing sentiment in favor of local governments ceasing to pay teachers' salaries—this function to be assumed by the national government. A leading educator in the Conservative Party, Dr. Kathleen Ollerenshaw, expressed her opposition to the idea and was supported by the *Times Educational Supplement,* especially in her argument that reducing the existing level of local responsibility for financing education "would turn teachers into civil servants, diminish local loyalties and eventually lessen the ties between teachers and the local community, the parents and the children whom they teach."[15]

Similar concern about the erosion of local responsibility for education exists in the United States, but recent court cases (for example the California case of Serrano V. Priest) have spotlighted the situation where one local school district spends twice as much money per school child as another school district in the same state. The courts are moving toward a requirement that all districts provide roughly the same amount of money per child; this would call for sizable increases in educational grants from the fifty state governments. This would still leave vast differences in educational expenditures between the fifty states, which leads a growing number of groups to urge more federal financing. The National Education Association, in 1972, suggested that 33 percent of school funds should come from the federal government instead of the current figure of 7 percent.

Shortages of educational funds continue to plague schools in England, and the national government periodically is forced to take drastic steps. In 1969 the government put a 3-1/2 percent ceiling on increases which LEAs could make over the previous year's expenditures, withdrawing national support of the free milk program for schools, and delaying several times the effective date for rising the compulsory school attendance age from 15 to 16. Hardly anyone in England challenges the right of the national government to act in such areas. The same was not true, however, when in the 1960s the national government entered the curriculum area.

Curriculum

No one denied the right of the national government to send its inspectors to see what was being taught in the schools. But in the twentieth century these visits had become less and less frequent, and great tact was exercised by the HMIs in commenting on what was being taught and how it was being taught. This is not to say that there was no pressure associated with these visits, but after two or three days the inspectors left and the LEA was free to make such changes as it deemed desirable.

The official view, promulgated well into the 1960s, was one of non-interference by the national government.

> Under the public system of education in England and Wales, the Ministry [of Education] does not issue directives or instructions about the curricula or syllabuses to be used in schools. Such matters are left to the local education authorities who are responsible for running the schools, and, in practice head teachers and staff are left fairly free to arrange their own curricula, syllabuses and schemes of work for the schools in their care.[16]

At the same time the national government had decided to play a more aggressive role in the curriculum area. In 1960 the Minister of Education announced in Parliament that he would try to have the Ministry of Education's voice heard more in regard to what was taught in schools and colleges. Two years later the Ministry established its own Curriculum Study Group without prior consultation with the teachers organizations.[17] Prior consultation had always been an important part of the old arrangement of control sharing—the partnership.

The National Union of Teachers and the Association of Education Committees reacted angrily and interpreted the move as a shift in the power arrangement.[18] The executive secretary of the latter group immediately spoke publicly of the potential dangers of national control.

> That he [Minister of Education] has chosen to establish a Curriculum Study Group at the Ministry, and that there has been no consultation with local education authorities and teachers before the group was established, is a matter of grave concern. Nor is it

enough that the Minister gives assurances that he will seek the cooperation of local education authorities and teachers in the tasks to be undertaken.

No one suggests that at the present time the Minister or Ministry are seeking powers of control and direction in matters of curriculum, but it is important that the machinery now established should safe-guard the future. Work undertaken by the Curriculum Study Group on the directions of the Minister and results conveyed to the schools by a Minister could give an authority which could subsequently lead to complete control and direction.[19]

The Minister of Education's justifications for intervening in the curriculum area were: 1) the rapidly changing society called for educational changes (presumably the local government and individual teachers were not capable of coping with such changes); 2) dissatisfaction with the current educational system; and 3) his view that stronger control and leadership were called for.[20]

The Curriculum Study Group in 1963 was absorbed into the newly-formed Schools Council for the Curriculum and Examinations, known commonly now as the Schools Council. In typical English fashion this was a private body supported by public funds and included representatives from the local governments, the national government, and the teachers' organizations.

Apparently the outcry from the National Union of Teachers and the Association of Education Committees had been heard; the Schools Council was to be a free association of the partners and would report to all the partners, not just to the national government. Teachers were to be a majority on the Council, and it would offer only recommendations.[21]

Attitudes toward the Schools Council over the years have varied. Manzer asserts that the Council did not become a group of high-powered researchers with startlingly new ideas which would lead education in new directions. Instead, the more conservative elements prevailed, and the stress has been on careful, limited experimentation. Generally the tendency has been to improvise within existing practices. The Council did, however, insure public scrutiny of curriculum and the national government now has a hand in that scrutiny via its representatives on the Council. So the national government emerged with a stronger influence on curriculum than before. Since non-educators are not represented, control remains with the established groups in education, namely the teachers' organizations, the Department of Education and Science, and the Education Committees of the LEAs.[22]

Professor A. D. C. Peterson, a leading educator in the Liberal Party, is favorably disposed and describes the Schools Council as an independent body representing the teaching profession as a whole. He sees the Council as purely advisory with no powers to impose and apparently no desire to impose. He approves particularly of the fact that the Council has entered into research, unlike its predecessors.[23]

Some of the research of the Schools Council takes place in Teacher Centers which sprang up in the late 1960s under stimulus from the Schools Council. A group of interested teachers form a Center and secure the use of a room or two in an existing school building during after-school hours or on Saturdays. According to some reports these are teacher-run operations and represent a trend of teachers controlling curriculum change.

In some cases the Teacher Centers seem to be no more than convenient places for teachers to take in-service courses; in some cases these are courses which the teachers suggested and in other instances ones proposed by LEA inspectors, or the national government inspectors.

There are signs also that some of the Teacher Centers are just places for carrying out projects designed by foundations, by the Department of Education and Science, and especially by the Schools Council. It is an open question as to how many of the activities of the Teacher Centers developed independently of publications, projects and suggestions of the Schools Council.

By its choice of projects to fund, the Schools Council

influences the priorities in education. Thus, in 1972 it drew attention to the growing racial problem in England (related to the influx of what the English call colored people from Pakistan, India, Jamaica and Africa) by allotting £126,500 (approximately $300,000) to a project "to help teachers to encourage in their pupils rational attitudes in race relations."

There has been some fear expressed that the influence of the Schools Council may have undermined the traditional freedom of the teacher in England to choose his own materials. The Council has published all kinds of materials relating to this or that subject in the curriculum, and the fear is that teachers are being subtly pressured into using these materials.

Those on the Council claim that teacher control of the Council is a reality and that earlier fears of national government dominance have proved unwarranted, especially under the new system whereby the national government's share of financing the Council has been reduced. As of April 1, 1970, half of the Council's money comes from local governments and half from the national government. The Council is portrayed by those on the Council as "the most powerful force for decentralization and pluralism in British education today." [24] It is worth noting that the national government's intervention in the area of curriculum seems to have generated curriculum reforms and an agency to promote pluralism.

Not everyone is satisfied with the pluralism of the Schools Council. One of the prominent organizations representing school administrators (the Headmasters Conference) denounced, in 1972, what it called the dominance of the Schools Council by NUT. [25] NUT has 17 of the 73 members of the Council, or roughly one-fourth of the total. The national government has four representatives. Other groups represented in the Council include the LEAs, other teachers' organizations besides NUT, universities, the Church of England, and the Catholic Education Council. Defenders of the Schools Council argue that if it is dominated by anything it is the desire to introduce innovation and reform into education and that any influence which the Council may have stems from the validity of the research which it encourages.

Research

The national government's interest in research prior to the 1960s had been largely limited since World War II to annual grants of a few thousand dollars to a handful of researchers organized as the National Foundation for Educational Research, a private body. In 1961, however, the national government entered directly into research by establishing the Research and Intelligence Branch in the Ministry of Education. About the same time, increasingly larger research grants were given to the National Foundation for Educational Research, to universities, and to teachers' organizations. In 1962 the grant to the National Foundation for Educational Research was the equivalent of $19,000; in 1964 it had grown to $300,000. At the same time, private foundations (notably the Nuffield Foundation), supplied small but increasing amounts of money for educational research.

The need for educational research had been dramatized by two national studies of education, the Crowther Report of 1959 on the 15- to 18-year-old group and the Robbins Report of 1963 on higher education. Both reports had complained of the lack of research on which to base policy decisions. Grants from the national government continued to grow throughout the 1960s, with little noticeable attempt to exercise national control over the research.

A change in policy became evident, however, in December 1970 when Mrs. Margaret Thatcher, head of the Department of Education and Science, announced that the national government was going to take a hand in the direction of educational research. Instead of just approving or disapproving research proposals submitted by independent researchers, the national government was now going to specify areas in need of research. She called this a change from a posture of patronage to one of commissioning research. The Department of Education and Science also would specify timetables for the completion of research. In this way research findings would be available for policy formation when the national government needed it. In typical English fashion, Mrs. Thatcher spoke of the new arrangement as a partnership of the government and the researchers. The benefit to the researcher, as she saw it, was that his findings would be used in policy formation.

The national government's new posture was in contrast to the continual erosion of initiative from the local level. In April 1972 Dame Kathleen Ollerenshaw, a long-time champion of local control, urged LEAs to initiate their own research projects—possibly with national government funds—but designed to solve local problems.[26]

Local Education Authorities may have trouble asserting themselves in the area of educational research since LEAs, unlike some large American school districts, don't maintain a staff of researchers. Most of the researchers are in the universities where they have enjoyed considerable freedom, including the freedom to ignore the problems of local schools. There are signs that the national government will no longer allow higher education to remain free of official scrutiny.

Higher Education

One would expect the least amount of government interference in the case of higher education, especially the university sector which prides itself on its autonomy. The universities, however, are increasingly less able to support themselves from tuition fees and endowment income. Over 70 percent of current operating costs and 90 percent of the funds for new buildings come from the national government.

Signs of Growing Centralized Control

The possibility of governmental supervision increased in 1964 when higher education was added to the responsibilities of the newly-formed Department of Education and Science. A sign of what was to come occurred in 1961 when the national government tried to eliminate the variations between LEAs in the size of scholarship grants for higher education. This was viewed by the LEAs as another step toward centralization.

The Labor Party in the interest of equality favored centralization. In 1963 it promised that if it came into office it would use national government power to regulate the upper-middle and upper-class tone of Oxford and Cambridge universities—specifically, tuition fees would be abolished, along with the entrance procedures which were viewed as favoring applicants from certain secondary schools and certain socio-economic groups. [27] Particularly under attack was the use of the interview to select new students. As Davis points out, professors at Oxbridge (Oxford and Cambridge) tended to have a private school background and unconsciously preferred the same kind of background in secondary school applicants.

> While, then, interviews are frequently conducted by the products of the "establishment" schools and background, it seems likely that, with the best will in the world, the qualities which they look for will be found most easily in boys from the same backgrounds as themselves. It must in justice be added that many Oxbridge colleges are seriously concerned because they admit so few boys from under-privileged homes and schools. A system which appears to tolerate or perpetuate social injustice is hardly likely to last long in the second half of the twentieth century. Those few colleges which maintain methods of selection which are not open to the light of day, and which are based upon the predilections of an individual don for potential 'blues' or members of certain families or schools, would be well advised to reconsider their methods.[28]

By the 1970s it was being suggested that higher entry qualifications should be demanded of middle-class children than of working-class children since an equivalent academic level achieved by the latter with their cultural handicaps suggested greater ability. It was also noted that even though the share of university enrollment taken by working-class children had risen in the 1960s, only one-third of the students in universities came from working-class homes.[29]

In 1966 the national government entered the tuition area by urging the universities to raise tuition fees for foreign students. All the universities then raised the tuition for foreign students except Oxford, Cambridge, and Bradford.

Until 1968 the national government had no accurate way of checking on how its grants of funds to the universities had been used. In 1968 the national government ordered that henceforth the universities would make their records available to the Comptroller and Auditor General for regular scrutiny. Previously the division of national funds among the universities, and any checks on the use of the money, was done by the University Grants Committee (UGC), a private group of professors and university administrators appointed by the national government but by tradition relatively free of government interference. By the end of the 1960s it was being suggested that UGC had been transformed into an advisory board serving the Department of Education and Science.[30] In this new relationship the Department of Education and Science set policy and informed the UGC, which passed the word back to the universities.

In 1969 the head of the university branch in the Department of Education and Science tried to allay fears of government interference by spelling out the role of the national government. In his view the actual legal powers of the Department of Education and Science over the universities were limited. The Department's chief job was to receive the budgetary requests from the UGC and return it "plus—or more likely minus—a few million pounds." He stressed that the national government had no right to intervene if one university was unhappy with its share of the block grant to the universities for operating expenses. It was a different story in regard to grants for buildings:

> The building programme is difficult. Here the Government has a good deal more information about the plans of the individual universities. This closer control is necessary because the building programme is always a case of stretching a limited amount of money as far as possible.[31]

He also pointed out that in spite of the theory of university autonomy the national government was involved in some of the important decisions made about universities. For example, the national government decides on the proportion of undergraduate students to graduate-level students, though with the advice of the UGC. The national government also decides in special situations, such as the decision to expand the number of medical students in the 1960s after a report of a national commission made this recommendation. When asked if national government restrictions on the universities had increased he admitted that this was so, but stressed that the traditional English procedure of consulting with all interested parties was still functioning well.

After reporting these views of the Department of Education and Science, the *Times Educational Supplement* editorialized that the universities were becoming more dependent on the national government for finances, and that the new universities were almost completely dependent. Moreover, it was less and less realistic to speak of universities as independent when the national government decided such policies as the percentage of students in residence, the balance of undergraduate to graduate students, and the number of staff. Control over student grants, it was speculated, could control what universities teach and "in this situation, advice and suggestion can chameleon-like suddenly appear as orders and commands."[32]

In other sectors of higher education, such as technical institutions, the power of the national governor is undisguised. Thus, in 1966 the national government chose 30 out of the 500 technical colleges and elevated them to the rank of "polytechnics" with authorization to offer more advanced work. In the United States the better institutions would have emerged over a period of time; it is also probable that a good many more than 30 would have attempted to offer the advanced work.

The polytechnics as they developed in England had to have their programs and courses approved by the Department of Education and Science. Some programs have been turned down because they failed to fit priorities established by the national government. One such priority area was management education, or business administration as it is called in the United States.

As England became aware of its lagging economy, in the 1960s more and more attention was given to the lack of up-to-date, imaginative executives in commerce and industry. The Robbins Report in 1963 drew attention to the problem, and the national government soon after picked out two universities to begin programs in management education. In 1969 a study of the problem was made by the national government's National Economic Development Office, and its report recommended that the national government triple the number of students in management education in the next six years. There was no questioning of the right of the national government to set such priorities.[33]

Ordinarily in the United States an expansion of a field of study would occur piecemeal as this or that university decided to expand a particular field, usually after popular and scholarly articles had dramatized the need. A notable exception occurred in the late 1950s when federal funds were offered to universities which were willing to expand language and foreign area programs. The same thing occurred in the area of science through grants from the National Science

Signs of Growing Centralized Control

Foundation. Since agencies of the federal government decided which universities would receive the grants there was a measure of national control operating.

In the late 1960s student protest activities in higher education further encouraged the growth of national power in England. Protest activities, though less disruptive than in France or the United States, led to a proposal that a Higher Education Commission be established to supervise the universities and to investigate protests. The students themselves, through their National Union of Students, encouraged intervention by the national government to conduct inquiries at institutions undergoing protest disruptions. The students said that they had no confidence in inquiries conducted by the institutions of higher education.

In the case of the polytechnics the national government issued an order in 1969 to the effect that henceforth a committee composed equally of students and faculty would be responsible for deciding the possible dismissal of a student. Two years later, when the forces of reaction had set in, the national government's Privy Council refused to approve Lancaster University's proposal to amend its governing statutes to add students to the governing board. The Privy Council asserted that the number of students to be added was too high.[34]

Controls over institutions of higher education often are justified in terms of the need to economize. For example, in the fall of 1969 the Department of Education and Science sent a letter to all colleges of education, both public and private, stating that the ratio of students to faculty must conform to a standard specified by the national government. Apparently wide differences had existed, with some colleges having a ratio of 7-1/2 students per faculty member and others as high as 12-1/2 per faculty member. Economy rather than standardization seems to have been the reason for the directive since the better staffed colleges were told to increase the number of students per faculty member.[35]

The economy move affected the universities as well. In 1970 the national government made it clear that the growing expansion of university enrollment would have to be accompanied by measures designed to reduce the cost of educating a given number of students. The Secretary of the Department of Education and Science even presented the universities in 1970 with a list of thirteen suggested ways to make more efficient use of buildings and staff to lessen the cost of the expansion of enrollments. The vice chancellors of the universities reacted strongly by rejecting all thirteen suggestions, but they came up with suggestions of their own. Moreover, the vice chancellors did not challenge the right of the national government to decide whether the expanding enrollments will be absorbed by existing institutions or by building new universities. In the United States the dynamics of public versus private, of expanding religious interests, of states' rights, of institutional aggrandizement, and the like, largely determine which institutions will grow to meet existing needs. In England, the national government decides.

The economy pressures from the national government in England are regarded by the Association of Vice Chancellors, and by the Association of University Teachers, as a tactic to make the universities amenable either to government cutbacks in funds, or, more likely, amenable to the national government increasing its grants more slowly than enrollments expand. A doubling of university enrollment in this decade is widely predicted.

The national government has succeeded in focusing attention on economy, and educational journals are filled with articles about the pros and cons of efficiency and the possible injury to academic standards and university traditions.

One attempt of the national government to achieve a more efficient arrangement of higher education was a notable failure. It began with the Robbins Report on higher education in 1963. The report recommended that the teachers' colleges (called colleges of education) be taken from the LEAs and turned over to the national government. The thought was that the transfer would free the colleges from the heavy-handed administration and parochial outlook of county governments. As the national government indicated a willingness to proceed with the recommendation, an outcry of protest came from defenders of local government. The national government then discretely decided not to implement that particular recommendation of the Robbins Report.

Colleges of education and most of the technical institutions on higher education levels are run by the local governments. In the late 1960s a trend developed toward greater freedom for these institutions—i.e., greater opportunity for the board of governors in each institution to be free of restrictions imposed by the county governments. Much of this freedom was delegated to the president of the institution (often he is called the principal). Interestingly enough, this new institutional freedom was ordered in 1967 by the national government via Circular 2/67 which told the colleges of education that they should reorganize their governing boards to conform to the recommendations of a study done in 1966 (Weaver Report).[36] Even so, many things, such as staff appointments and new courses, have to approved by the LEA. The amount of control exercised over the institutions varies from one LEA to another.

In the 1970s demands have grown for more coordination of the various institutions of higher education and the various sectors (universities, colleges of education, polytechnics, and so on). In 1970 a report of the House of Commons Select Committee on Education called for more financing of higher education by the national government and more coordination from the national level.[37] The need for coordination is a reasonable, and often used, argument for more action by the national government. Even the National Union of Teachers in its publication *Into the 70's* called on the Department of Education and Science to set a national policy for higher education.[38]

The universities are not likely to welcome any further intrusions by the national government and their views are well-represented by Sir Sidney Caine, former head of the London School of Economics:

> ... given the political structure of this country it is highly unlikely that state [national government] intervention will be inspired by anything deeper than efficiency, economy and the serving of short-term political ends. Universities have best served their most basic purposes of being ... when they have been independent of government and inspired by some vital and independent philosophy.[39]

The universities complain about growing interference by the national government, but in fact their autonomy is still intact and the universities continued to ignore many national needs. One weapon open to the national government is in the area of salaries of professors. The national government establishes the salary scales for university professors and recently has talked of the need to bring such salaries into line with salaries in other occupations. There is no machinery for negotiation, but the Association of University Professors is agitating for the establishment of such machinery. There has long existed machinery for the negotiation of salaries of elementary and secondary teachers but it has not been invulnerable to national government pressure.

Salaries

Since 1919 salaries of teachers for all of England have been set by the Burnham Committee in order to avoid local areas competing with each other for scarce teachers. Until the 1960s the Burnham Committee consisted of representatives of the local governments on one side and representatives of various teachers' organizations on the other side; the national government was not represented officially. The Minister of Education (later Secretary of the Department of Education and Science) had to approve the salary scale, but for a long time this was done in a kind of rubber stamp fashion.

Twice in the 1950s when the negotiations reached an impasse the National Union of Teachers asked the Ministry of Education to intervene. So in the 1960s when the national government decided to intervene on its own, the precedents were there. Apparently the national government decided to take a hand in the negotiations in the 1960s partly because the local governments were not holding the line against salary increases and because England's future as a leading nation was increasingly seen as dependent on careful and efficient use of all its resources. The latter called for some kind of national coordination.

Beginning in 1961 the national government pushed hard for a larger and more public role in the Burnham Committee negotiation. NUT, which had a majority of the teacher representatives on the Burnham Committee, reacted angrily and called for a march of 10,000 teachers to lobby Parliament while in session. When the Minister of Education firmly rejected the salary scale agreed to by local authorities and teachers' groups on the Burnham Committee, teachers' strikes occurred in London and several other regions, and NUT talked about a nationwide strike.

In 1963 the Minister of Education again angered the teachers, not only by rejecting the Burnham Committee agreement, but by taking the unusual step of sending his own salary plan to the Burnham Committee for consideration. After a motion to censure the government failed of passage in Parliament, a law was passed which in effect allowed the Minister of Education to determine the salary scale. Meanwhile newspapers and journals were filled with charges and countercharges on the issue of the proper role of the national government.

Compulsory arbitration entered the picture in 1965 by an act of Parliament which made the national government an official member of the management side of the Burnham Committee and ended the requirement that any agreement had to have the approval of the Department of Education and Science (formerly Ministry of Education). In the event of an impasse in negotiations, the salary scale was to be set by an outside tribunal appointed by the national government's Ministry of Employment.

By 1969 there was growing criticism of the way the Burnham Committee was functioning, especially the way in which the national government had assumed the role of dominant partner on the management side. One suggestion that received publicity in the newspapers called for the retention of a national scale as a minimum, but would allow local negotiations with individual LEAs to secure payments above the national scale.[40]

The teachers' organizations became increasingly militant as the steady growth of inflation made sizable salary increases a must in their eyes. Strikes against individual LEAs occurred as ways of indicating displeasure with existing salaries. The national government in turn adopted a posture of toughness in trying to keep the salaries of the various occupations within the limits which the national economy could bear. As a final weapon the national government threatened to use its Price and Income Board to invalidate salary raises set by the Burnham Committee.

The Burnham Committee after 1965 frequently failed to reach an agreement, and outside arbitration was used repeatedly. In June 1972 the Association of Education Committees, representing the views of local governments, complained that outsiders rather than the Burnham Committee were making the decisions on salaries. Moreover, the 1971 arbitration award was 2 percent higher than what the management side of the Burnham Committee had offered. In 1972 the arbitration board again set a salary scale above what the local governments and the national government had proposed.

The Association of Education Committees urged that the procedures be changed to get rid of the national government from the bargaining table and to end outside arbitration. The local government claimed that their powers had been eroded since 1965 and they had become errand boys for the national government in the salary negotiations.[41]

Less Visible Powers

The national government's flexing of its muscles in the salary area was out in the open for all to see. In fact there is some evidence to indicate that the national government publicized its moves so that the issue of national government participation in the salary area would be seen as a possibility. In many other areas, however, the national government has moved quietly to extend—or assert—its power while pledging its continued allegiance to the tradition of local autonomy.

In 1965 when the national government established a five-year plan for economic development of the nation it did not consult teachers or their organizations in regard to the education part of the plan. Later in the 1960s the national government said no to a request from the teachers' organizations that a Teachers' Council be established to decide who would be allowed to teach—the Council was to be run by elected representatives of the teachers. It is significant that in England the teachers felt that they should ask the national government. The government's refusal was not surprising since the trend is probably in the other direction—i.e., away from control by the professionals and toward more public supervision of the professionals.[42]

The national government, in fact, in the late 1960s reasserted its powers to fire teachers in public or private schools by issuing a circular to "clarify" its powers. The *Times Educational Supplement* hailed the step as necessary and desirable.

> Some recent controversial cases have focused attention on the Secretary of State's statutory right to restrict the employment of teachers whom he has judged guilty of professional misconduct.

Now the Department has issued a circular announcing the intention of strengthening the Minister's hand by ironing out some troublesome technical minutiae. The need for control needs to be restated. Children must be protected and before the present system there were far too many examples of undesirables gaining employment in the schools—particularly in the then uncontrolled private sector.[43]

If the same powers resided with the federal government in 1968 in the United States, President Johnson, or the Secretary of HEW, could have fired the Negro teacher in New York City who read a poem to his class denouncing Jews.

Even the private schools in England not receiving public tax funds are subject to some control by the national government. The Act of 1944 gave the national government the right, and the duty, to inspect "every educational establishment" at intervals deemed by the Ministry of Education as appropriate. For a long time the national government made only feeble efforts to inspect the private schools. As late as 1962, only 1500 of the 4000 private schools had been inspected and given the label "recognized as efficient."[44] In the late 1960s, however, the Department of Education and Science announced a policy of closing down all private schools which failed to meet national standards. In 1969 twenty-eight of the HMIs were assigned part-time to inspect the remaining 2000 private schools not recognized as "efficient." Occasionally a school was put out of business, as was the case with a Jewish school in 1970; the school reportedly devoted too much time to religion and too little to secular subjects.[45]

Aggressive government action against the 100 or so most famous private schools (called "public schools" in England) was threatened throughout the 1960s but failed to materialize. They were subjected to a searching scrutiny by an ad hoc committee appointed by the national government; the report came out in 1968. Defenders of these private schools described the inquiry as a straight power play by the national government to control the development of private education.[46]

The Labor Party had long threatened to use governmental power to close or absorb the private schools when it came into power. Once in power in the 1960s, the Labor Party failed to take decisive action against the private schools—to which, incidentally, many of the children of Labor Party leaders were going. In 1969 NUT called for an end to all private schools and for greater powers for the national government so that it could close private schools not meeting the national standards.[47]

Defenders of the private schools equated their continuance with preservation of freedom and individual choice.

> There are already too many dangers of coercion and control by central government, too many restrictions on what we can do with our money or choose for our lives. It is also clear that the abolition of private schools would entail sanctions of a kind still barely contemplated, and wholly at odds with freedom of choice.[48]

In the 1970s there is still talk of closing the private schools, but the national government has backed off from such action.

The national government has not hesitated, however, to overrule local governmental authorities in regard to county schools. This was the case in 1970 when the Education Committee of the Brighton LEA refused to let the younger son in a particular family go to the same school as his older brother; the latter had been assigned to a school out of his district for reasons of health. When the mother appealed directly to the national government the Department of Education and Science ruled in favor of the mother.[49]

Educational Priority Areas

In effect, the national government in England has come to be the judge of what is right or wrong, important or unimportant in education. This is clearly seen in the 1970s in governmental efforts to help poor and disadvantaged children. The plan is that the national government will spend extra money on those children doing poorly in school, especially those living in slum areas. The term Educational Priority Areas (EPA) is used both to designate the sections of cities where the schools and homes are inadequate and to indicate which level of education will get major attention.

The national government decides which are to be the EPAs, and in the 1970s—thanks to mounting interest in both the United States and England in the early years of child rearing—nursery schools and nursery age activities have been picked. In making its choice the national government was aware, of course, of the flood of articles by educators and psychologists on the value of nursery education, to say nothing of resolutions passed by NUT and lobbying activities of citizen groups formed to promote nursery education. Actually the national government says its major focus is on elementary education, which has been redefined by the national government to include nursery education. Interestingly enough it was the national government in 1960 which called a halt to nursery school expansion with its Circular 8/60 which enjoined LEAs from adding additional facilities for nursery education. In 1964 the same policy of low priority for nursery school expansion was reiterated by the national government.[50]

Educational Priority Areas are receiving considerable attention in England, but at a conference on Social Deprivation and Change in Education, in April 1972, serious questions were raised about the national government's proper role. For example, discussion centered around the question, "will central government intervention in the distribution of financial resources at local level be more likely to work than local authority discretion," or "should the focal point be the assertiveness of the local community?"[51]

Similar questions have been asked in the United States, especially after the federal government in the 1960s began to take a hand in setting educational priorities. Bayard Rustin of the Civil Rights movement has noted this new governmental activity with approval.

> ... not only did the courts prod government to pursue the total desegregation of Southern schools, but government [federal] itself, acting with broad popular support, participated in the establishment of educational priorities for the first time. Flawed as they may have been, the innovative and compensatory programs of the Johnson administration represented the first substantive effort to overcome both the legally sanctioned inequality of dual school systems and the de facto inequality of an economic order weighted to the affluent and well-educated.[52]

Requests for Intervention

Increasingly the national government in England is becoming more active, partly because so many different groups ask for national government intervention in educational disputes. This was the case as protest activities by students in secondary schools and institutions of higher education attracted public attention at the end of the 1960s. At one secondary school. Kingsdale School in Dulwich, five students were suspended at the beginning of 1970 for joining a one-day strike led by a national organization called Schools Action Union. The headmaster's action of suspending the students was narrowly upheld by the board of governors for the school. The parents then contacted the Department of Education and Science and asked it to intervene.[53] Obviously the parents saw the national government as having the power to decide such matters.

In the case of student protest at the higher education level, militant students repeatedly called on the national government to intervene and conduct an investigation of this or that institution. One of the top officials in the Department of Education and Science finally spoke up in January 1970 and said that it would be improper, and probably illegal, for the national government to intervene in the affairs of a single institution of higher education.[54]

When the heads of the technical colleges at the end of the 1960s became dissatisfied with the way that the Industrial Training Act of 1964 was working, they said, through their association, that the remedy is "firmer control at the national level," and referred specifically to the Department of Education and Science.[55] The latter was criticized for no longer having firm control over technical education.

The Department of Education and Science was criticized by the big labor union federation (the Trades Union Congress—TUC) in 1969 for not exercising its powers over the LEAs. TUC also urged that the powers of LEA be curtailed, and those of the Department of Education and Science expanded.[56] Actions by the National Union of Teachers also encouraged national government intervention—apparently NUT prefers a national system of education to a real local system.[57]

In 1968, in testimony before Parliament's Select Committee on Education, NUT urged that the Department of Education and Science direct the HMIs to inspect and rate LEAs in terms of whether they were progressive or backward in providing education.[58]

A year later NUT urged that the Department of Education and Science be given the power to force each LEA to establish a strong Education Committee, one which included teacher representatives, and that no LEA Education Committee be allowed to function unless the national government had given its approval as to the powers and composition of the Committee.[59]

The advice of the national government is sought even on little things. For instance, in the spring of 1970, a member of Parliament rose and asked the Department of Education and Science to send advice to the LEAs on how to handle the problem of a shortage of hard coke for the school furnaces. A high-ranking official in the Department replied that the national government was prepared to grant funds to local governments to make alterations in the furnaces.[60]

Members of Parliament make frequent requests that the Department of Education and Science intervene in this or that way. No doubt they feel that they are representing their constituents in making such requests, but the overall effect is to encourage centralized power. At times the Department of Education and Science resists the temptation to exercise control over the LEAs. This was the case in May 1971 when a member of Parliament asked the Secretary of the Department of Education and Science to order all LEAs to spend as much on school books as the figure recommended by the Association of Education Committees. The Secretary's reply was that the national government was concerned but this was a matter for the LEAs to handle.[61]

In July 1971, a member of Parliament asked the Department of Education and Science to direct the LEAs to issue guidelines on suitable clothing for school—such guidelines to apply to all schools in the LEA rather than leaving such matters to the discretion of the individual headmaster. The Department declined to do this on the grounds that this was LEA business.[62]

One year later the Department of Education and Science was asked by a member of Parliament to order all LEAs not to worsen the pupil-teacher ratio. The reply of the Secretary of the Department of Education and Science stated that it was up to the LEAs to keep class size down, but she hoped that there would be no cutting back on the number of teachers.[63] The same week another member of Parliament asked the Secretary to insist that each LEA guarantee each teacher the right to take one year off, with pay, for further study at least once during his career. The Secretary agreed to check into the matter.[64]

If an educational issue becomes hot enough it eventually reaches the doorstep of the national government. This was the case with the so-called "violence in the schools" issue. By violence the English meant not just unruly pupils, but also numerous instances of pupils striking teachers. By 1972 the militant association of men teachers, the National Association of Schoolmasters, had mounted a campaign to get government action to curb such violence. NUT at first tried to play down the issue, but finally the national government agreed in April to check with the LEAs to determine the extent of the problem and possible remedies.[65] In June at the annual meeting of the National Association of Headteachers, a resolution was endorsed which called on the Department of Education and Science to act on the matter of school violence.

> If this is a national problem, a national undertaking should act. It is the job of the Department of Education and Science.[66]

Advisory Commissions

Occasionally the national government chooses to handle a national educational problem by appointing a national commission or committee to make a study of the issue. The report of the commission is published by the national government.

The Education Act of 1944 gave the national government vast powers, but it also established advisory commissions as a device to keep watch on the national government. The most important of these, the Central Advisory Council, is composed of knowledgeable citizens appointed by the national government.

Unlike its predecessor, the Consultative Committee of the old national Board of Education, the Central Advisory Council could initiate studies and investigations on its own. In practice, the national government has initiated the inquiries, often after much pressure from certain groups in society, and assigned the task to the Central Advisory Council.

Signs of Growing Centralized Control

The English tradition of surveys by national commissions goes back to the 1850s. England's success with these commissions reportedly was due to:

a) the existence of a group of dedicated citizens with time and interest to engage in a study of social questions;
b) the absence of administrative officials so specialized, and entrenched, as to resist change;
c) a degree of political and national stability so that public and open criticism is tolerated.[67]

In the second half of the 1960s the national government negated the advisory commission device by simply refusing to appoint persons to the commissions. Thus, the commission on the supply and training of teachers expired in 1965, and the same thing happened to the Central Advisory Council in the late 1960s.

In place of the advisory commissions the national government has appointed ad hoc committees to investigate a particular topic. In this way the national government exercises control over which areas will receive attention. Some persons claim that at times the national government uses ad hoc committees as a weapon. Thus, the committee appointed to study the famous private schools (called "public schools" in England) was described as "an overt political threat to their existence."[68]

Yet, the ad hoc committees, and the advisory commissions, reach their conclusions independently, and they are often critical of the very government which appointed them. At the same time, the national government finds the ad hoc committees useful in moving the country in a particular direction. The mere fact of appointing a committee of inquiry focuses attention on a specific sector of education and in a sense gives priority to it.

The report of the committee of inquiry inevitably shapes public opinion and results in pressures for change—including pressure on the national government itself. The latter, however, has considerable choice as to which parts of the committee's report it chooses to implement via grants of money and regulations as to the use of such money.

Some of the reports have been implemented more fully than others, but all of them are cited frequently by educators and government officials alike. The influence of these reports is difficult to measure precisely but must be sizable. The Plowden Report (*Children and their Primary Schools*) is a good example and will be discussed in depth in later chapters. The report was published in 1967, and by 1970 had sold 117,000 copies. It seems more than coincidence that in the period 1967-1972 the national government has:

a) given official recognition to the importance of the early years of schooling;
b) started an expansion of nursery school facilities and enrollment;
c) stressed parent participation in education;
d) increased the number of elementary schools which use the so-called open or free methods.

By refusing to appoint a commission of inquiry the national government also controls education by keeping the existing priorities and patterns in force. For example, in the late 1960s demands were made by educators and members of Parliament for a national commission to be appointed to investigate teacher training. The Department of Education and Science refused to appoint such a committee. Finally, in 1969-1970 a committee of Parliament (the Select Committee on Education and Science) started its own preliminary inquiry into the training of teachers "despite discouragement and resistance" from the Department of Education and Science. [69] Finally in 1971 the Department of Education and Science appointed the "James Committee" to investigate teacher education.

In a similar way the appointment of a commission in 1972 to study the teaching of reading came after a rising crescendo of criticism about the teaching of reading.

On the nagging comprehensive school question, the national government chose not to appoint a commission of inquiry. Instead, a decision was made by officials in the Department of Education and Science that comprehensive schools should be promoted, so a directive (Circular 10/65) to that effect was issued to the LEAs.

Secondary School Reorganization

The big controversy in England for the last ten years has been whether the bright students at the secondary school level should be segregated. By the mid-1960s a system of separate schools had developed whereby the top 20 percent of the students at age eleven were assigned to high-prestige academic secondary schools (grammar schools); 3 percent went to secondary technical schools of moderately good reputation; 6 percent avoided the whole problem by buying their way into private schools; and the remainder, roughly 70 percent, were assigned to the secondary modern school, which did not offer a full-length program (it ended at roughly the tenth grade, to use American terminology) and which had low prestige. Studies showed that the grammar school was largely an institution for middle-class children and that working-class children usually ended up in the secondary modern school.

The secondary modern school was widely known as the dumping ground (for 70 percent of the population); assignment to this school at age eleven meant that your station in life had been pretty well determined.

Critics of the system called for the establishment of comprehensive secondary schools where all students would go and where academic and vocational programs would be available under the same roof. The Labor Party showed considerable favor toward the comprehensive school, while the Conservative Party's view was that there was room for a few more comprehensive schools in certain areas (such as in new housing developments), but that the separate grammar schools were proven institutions and should not be abandoned.

Just before the October 1964 elections the Labor Party's spokesman on educational issues declared that his party placed great importance on ending social discrimination and on making fuller use of the untapped pool of talent. He added that the Labor Party did not want to "level down academic standards" or uproot all the grammar schools. The Labor Party did intend, he said, to encourage local areas to try out comprehensive schools.[70]

The Labor Party won the election, and in 1965 the national government applied pressure. Some reform was underway before the Labor Party exerted pressure, but not enough to satisfy the proponents of comprehensive schools.

> In January 1965 the view from Curzon Street [home of Department of Education and Science] was bewildering and exciting. Reorganization had suddenly become fashionable: 65 out of 148 local authorities had already drawn up a detailed plan to go more or less comprehensive, and another 55 were considering some kind of reorganization. But although the tide was moving... only a handful of authorities had yet coped with the hard practical problems of putting schemes into operation. In general, the school system was still the old class-ridden one of 1944. And... the reforming authorities were beginning to hit the submerged rocks in the way of reform.[71]

The national government applied pressure via Circular 10/65 which ordered all LEAs to submit plans for establishing comprehensive schools. Americans will notice the similarities to the desegregation of schools procedures used in the United States at this same time.

Contrary to the usual procedure of submitting a proposed policy change to teachers' organizations for comment, the Department of Education and Science issued Circular 10/65 without asking for comments from NUT or the other teachers' organizations. The Secretary of the Department of Education and Science did stress, however, that within any particular LEA teachers should be consulted with regard to the procedures for a change over to comprehensive schools. He did not suggest that teachers be consulted on the basic question of whether to change over to a system of comprehensive schools.[72]

The Labor Party moved cautiously in terms of pressuring the LEAs, and in 1968 some critics argued that the Department of Education and Science was still approving LEA plans which retained some degree of selection and segregation. Critics on the other side accused the national government of pushing too hard for comprehensive schools. In retrospect, the national government seemed to have been following an unofficial policy of settling for moderate but steady growth of comprehensives. Again the parallels with the integration of schools issue in the U.S. are striking.

At the annual meeting of the Labor Party in October 1968, a resolution was passed urging the national government to take stronger action to prevent "doctrinaire local authorities from destroying or delaying the introduction of comprehensive education."[73]

The Conservative Party also met in October 1968, and condemned the national government's attempts to force local education authorities to accept comprehensive schools.

> This conference condemns the Government's attempt to force on local education authorities, regardless of the wishes of parents and elected representatives, schemes of secondary school reorganization calculated to destroy established grammar schools, and to lower academic standards; and calls on the Conservative Party to give clear and unequivocal support to Conservative local authorities which seek, in persuance of their election pledges, to resist Government blackmail and preserve their grammar schools from senseless destruction.[74]

Between January 1965 and January 1969 the number of comprehensives rose from 262 to 962 and enrollments from

239,000 to 772,000—the latter figure representing roughly one-fourth of the students in secondary schools. By 1970 the comprehensive enrollments were 31 percent of the total.

Not all of the LEAs bowed to national government pressure in regard to comprehensive schools. In 1970 the Secretary of the Department of Education and Science reported that eight of the LEAs had refused to submit plans in accordance with Circular 10/65; five had even refused to acknowledge the circular; and nine LEAs whose plans were rejected by the national government did not resubmit plans. Thus, 22 LEAs out of 163 were refusing to cooperate.

Those LEAs which refused to join the comprehensive school movement sometimes cited their lack of money to build a series of comprehensive schools. Even more frequently they asserted the importance of preserving local control. They were supported by editorials in the *Times Educational Supplement* using such phrases as "the comprehensive school juggernaut."

The national government's approach with recalcitrant LEAs was to hold up approval of their school building program. The Secretary of the Department of Education and Science in 1969 reported that in the case of four of the LEAs she had given approval to their building program after the LEAs gave signs of moving toward comprehensive schools.

The City of Birmingham refused to be coerced and threatened a law suit unless the Department of Education and Science approved its building program in 1969. The Conservative Party had won control of the City Council in Birmingham with a pledge to "save the grammar schools."

At this point the national government publicly admitted that its legal powers to force LEAs were weak and asked Parliament for a new law strengthen the hand of the national government. The one weapon which the Department of Education and Science did have was that of withholding funds for school building by withholding approval of the plans. This resembled the actions of the U.S. Department of

Health, Education and Welfare as it pressured local school districts to desegregate under the threat of loss of federal funds. In the 1970s the executive branch of the federal government ceased to exert much pressure and left it to the courts to bring recalcitrant school districts into line.

The Conservative Party in England opposed the request for additional powers for the national government. The Conservatives promised that if elected to office they would repeal any law which forced LEAs to establish comprehensive schools. The Conservative Party argued that school organization should be left to local discretion, and any plan for secondary education which had the backing of parents and teachers would be accepted by the Conservative Party. The head of the Conservative Party added, however, that the national government would reserve the right to intervene if the plan was unsuitable.[75]

Even citizen groups favorable to comprehensive education were alarmed at the proposed extension of national government power. The Confederation for the Advancement of State Education, and its journal, *Parents and Schools,* was a good example.

> Sir—The Confederation for the Advancement of State Education, a body incorporating more than 100 local associations of parents and teachers, have long been in favour of a changeover to comprehensive secondary schooling.
>
> Nevertheless we share the opposition expressed in your leading article (May 16) to the Government's proposed legislation to compel all local authorities to submit schemes of reorganization for their schools. In our view, such legislation would be a further step towards more central control of education and would be restrictive of local authority experimentation—and we remember that comprehensive schools themselves started as local experiments.
>
> ... The Government would be wiser (a) to leave comprehensive schools as an issue to enliven local politics, and (b) to encourage

local authorities to "go comprehensive" by channelling more building allocations specifically for the purpose.[76]

At the same time, some members of the Labor Party criticized the national government for not being aggressive enough. It was noted that the famous Circular 10/65 had not specified what kind of secondary school pattern should be adopted except that it must encourage comprehensive schools. As a result there was much variation among the LEAs as to the age of transfer to secondary education, whether there was to be a lower secondary school, whether there was to be a selection and segregation process at the end of the lower secondary school, and so on. Even the *Times Educational Supplement* editorialized that little uniformity had been imposed by the national government.[77]

In 1970 the Conservative Party won the election. The Department of Education and Science promptly issued Circular 10/70 repealing Circular 10/65. The Secretary announced that the Department of Education and Science would no longer approve or disapprove of LEA plans to reorganize secondary education but would merely take note of them. In addition, LEA plans previously approved could be modified if the LEA requested. In a sense the national government was trying to control educational developments by not acting; the point, of course, was to slow down the comprehensive school trend.

The Department of Education and Science, in fact, did use its powers to approve and disapprove; proposed mergers of grammar schools with secondary modern schools to form a comprehensive school were viewed with a jaundiced eye. This was the case with the London borough of Barnet in 1972, which happened to be the Secretary's own borough. She opposed Barnet's proposed comprehensive school plan on technical grounds and because, she said, the public opposed it. Her term was "local objections." Later, in a speech before NUT, she defended this action and noted that in the previous year she had approved the plans of thirty areas seeking to introduce the comprehensive school pattern.[78]

Citizen opposition is often cited when the national government wishes to oppose a particular development. This was the case in April 1972 when the Department of Education and Science vetoed a proposed merger of St. Marylebone Grammar School and Rutherford Comprehensive School, giving "opposition of parents" as one of the reasons. Supporters of the merger claimed that it had the support of the headmaster, staff, and board of governors of the comprehensive school and the board of governors of the grammar school; opposing were the head of the grammar school and a substantial number of parents of grammar school pupils.[79]

Considerable citizen pressure existed in favor of comprehensive schools, as for example in the County of Buckinghamshire where a citizen organization called STEP (Stop The Eleven Plus examination) collected 21,000 signatures on a petition to end selection and establish comprehensive schools.[80]

Conservatives in England often claim that comprehensive schools are something a few at the top would like to impose on the unwilling majority at the local level. President Nixon took the same tact in regard to busing of students in a September 3, 1972, speech in which he said that the master planners who want more power in central government favor busing of school children to achieve racial balance.[81]

The comprehensive school issue is England's counterpart of America's busing issue. The power of the national government in England has been used alternately to speed up or to slow down the movement toward comprehensive schools, depending on the party in power.

The teachers' organizations in England have not stood idly by while the national government worked its will. They have sought to influence the comprehensive school issue, and other issues as well.

NOTES

1. W. O. Lester Smith, *Education in Great Britain,* fourth ed. London: Oxford Univ. Press, 1964, pp. 170-171.
2. David Wardle, *English Popular Education, 1780-1970.* London: Cambridge Univ. Press, 1970, p. 154.
3. W. O. Halls, *Society, Schools and Progress in France.* New York: Pergamon, 1965, p. 74.
4. Ronald A. Manzer, *Teachers and Politics in England and Wales.* Toronto, Can.: Univ. of Toronto Press, 1970, pp. 23-25.
5. Edmund J. King, *Other Schools and Ours,* third ed. New York: Holt, Rinehart and Winston, 1967, pp. 103-112.
6. Edmund J. King, "Comparative Studies," p. X in John J. Figueroa, *Society, Schools and Progress in the West Indies.* New York: Pergamon, 1971.
7. Wardle, op. cit., p. 153.
8. Ibid.
9. Manzer, op. cit., pp. 5-6.
10. Times Educational Supplement (London), June 22, 1962, p. 1257.
11. Ibid.
12. John Vaizey, *Britain in the Sixties: Education for Tomorrow.* London: Penguin, 1962, p. 100.
13. Times Educational Supplement (London), June 14, 1963, p. 1289.
14. Ibid., April 23, 1965, p. 1245.
15. Ibid., March 36, 1965, p. 897.
16. British Ministry of Education. *England and Wales: Educational Developments in 1962-63.* London: Her Majesty's Stationery Office, 1963, pp. 9-10. As late as 1971 scholars in England were still echoing the official line that the national government had relatively little to do with curriculum; for example see Maurice Kogan, *The Government of Education.* New York: Citation, 1971, p. 15.
17. Manzer, op. cit., p.91.
18. Ibid., p. 93.
19. Sir William Alexander, "Comments On the Address Given by D. H. Morrell." Educational Research, Vol. 5, Feb. 1963, p. 91.
20. Manzer, op. cit., p. 92.
21. Ibid., p. 95.
22. Ibid., pp. 95-97.
23. A. D. C. Peterson, "Educational Reform in England and Wales, 1955-1966." Comparative Education Review, Vol. XI, No. 3, Oct. 1967, p. 294.

24. Times Educational Supplement (London), April 10, 1970, p. 10.
25. Ibid., July 7, 1972, p. 5.
26. Ibid., April 14, 1972, p. 10.
27. Ibid., May 31, 1963, p. 1208.
28. Harry Davies, *Culture and the Grammar School.* London: Routledge and Kegan Paul, 1965, p. 145.
29. Times Educational Supplement (London), January 15, 1971, p. 6.
30. Sir Sidney Caine, *British Universities: Purpose and Prospects.* Toronto, Can.: Univ. of Toronto Press, 1969, pp. 188-192.
31. Times Educational Supplement (London), May 23, 1969, p. 1710.
32. Ibid.
33. Ibid., June 13, 1969, p. 1909.
34. Ibid., July 16, 1971, p. 3.
35. Ibid., October 31, 1969, p. 3.
36. William Taylor, *Society and the Education of Teachers.* London: Faber and Faber, 1969, p. 83.
37. Times Educational Supplement (London), January 16, 1970, p. 8.
38. National Union of Teachers. *Into the 70's.* London: NUT, 1969, pp. 30-32.
39. Sir Sidney Caine, op. cit., p. 266.
40. Times Educational Supplement (London), April 11, 1969, p. 1163.
41. Ibid., June 30, 1972, p. 1.
42. Norman Morris, "England," p. 76 in Albert A. Blum, ed., *Teacher Unions and Associations: A Comparative Study.* Urbana, Ill.: Univ. of Illinois Press, 1969.
43. Times Educational Supplement (London), January 23, 1968, p. 229.
44. British Ministry of Education. *Statistics for Education,* 1962, Part I. London: Her Majesty's Stationery Office, 1963, p. 30.
45. Times Educational Supplement (London), April 3, 1970, p. 12.
46. Ibid., April 10, 1970, p. 10. See statement by the president of the Independent School Association.
47. *Into the 70's,* op. cit., p. 33.
48. C. A. Cox and A. E. Dyson, eds. *The Black Papers on Education.* London: Davis-Poynter, 1971, p. 32.
49. Times Educational Supplement (London), July 16, 1971, p. 3.
50. John A. Griffith, *Central Departments and Local Authorities.* Toronto, Can.: Univ. of Toronto Press, 1966, p. 68.

51. Times Educational Supplement (London), April 14, 1972, p. 1.
52. Bayard Rustin, "Equal Opportunity and the Liberal Will." Washington Post, October 15, 1972, pp. B-1, B-4.
53. Times Educational Supplement (London), February 6, 1970, p. 5.
54. Ibid., January 16, 1970, p. 8.
55. Ibid., October 17, 1969, p. 10.
56. Ibid., May 2, 1969, p. 143.
57. Manzer, op. cit., p. 74.
58. John Blackie, *Inspecting and the Inspectorate*. London: Routledge and Kegan Paul, 1970, p. 61.
59. *Into the 70's*, op. cit., p. 24.
60. Times Educational Supplement (London), April 10, 1970.
61. Ibid., May 14, 1971, p. 12.
62. Ibid., July 16, 1971, p. 11.
63. Ibid., July 21, 1972, p. 10.
64. Ibid.
65. Ibid., April 14, 1972, p. 8.
66. Ibid., June 2, 1972, p. 3.
67. George Baron, *Society, Schools and Progress in England*. London: Pergamon, 1965, pp. 52-53.
68. Times Educational Supplement (London), June 23, 1972, p. 15.
69. Ibid., May 21, 1971, p. 2. Statement by Fred Willey (Labor MP).
70. Ibid., September 25, 1964, p. 457.
71. Anthony Sampson, *Anatomy of Britain Today*. New York: Harper and Row, 1965, p. 192.
72. Morris, op. cit., p. 71.
73. Times Educational Supplement (London), October 4, 1968, p. 684.
74. Ibid., October 11, 1968, p. 756.
75. Ibid., September 12, 1969, p. 28.
76. Ibid., May 23, 1969, p. 1725.
77. Ibid., June 12, 1970, p. 2.
78. Ibid., April 7, 1972, p. 5.
79. Ibid., April 21, 1972, p. 3.
80. Ibid., June 16, 1972, p. 10.
81. As reported in Washington Post, September 4, 1972, p. A-1.

Chapter 4

TEACHER POWER

In a sense teachers have always had power—the power to influence the individual lives of their students and through them the shape of the society. This kind of power, however, is difficult to see or measure and doesn't give teachers any sense of controlling their professional lives. Oftentimes, too, it fails to bring the normal amount of status and material security which professionals usually expect.

In terms of controlling their professional lives teachers have long been a group lacking in power. Writing in the 1960s, Jules Henry spoke of the continued vulnerability of teachers in the United States.

> There is no more vulnerable white collar group than educators. For the most part without unions, subject to the whims of principals, superintendents, boards of education and local parent organizations, elementary and high school teachers stand unprotected at the bottom of one of the most extended pyramids of power in the country.[1]

Teachers in England are harassed less than in the United States, partly because of a tradition of teacher autonomy and partly because of a lack of a tradition that schools and teachers should respond to the will of the people.

The American teacher has had less success against the deep-rooted radicalism of his society, which insists that its teachers, like its congressmen, shall recognize the sovereignty of the people. In Britain the people is not sovereign; and perhaps for this reason both teachers and parliamentarians have greater latitude, more freedom of manoeuvre. Of course they can be brought to book, but their work is not defined in detail by a mandate from the people whom they serve.[2]

Professional Associations

In both England and the United States teachers have formed organizations to guard their professional interests. In the United States the National Education Association was the chief organization at the national level until 1916 when the American Federation of Teachers was established. Until the 1920s the National Education Association disavowed militant tactics and hoped that by raising the level of education of teachers and improving the quality of teaching the public would award teachers status, material security and professional respect. After 50 or 60 years this approach obviously was not working.

The American Federation of Teachers was openly militant from the beginning, and by the 1940s the National Education Association was aggressively seeking to protect the rights of teachers. By the 1960s both groups were using strikes, boycotts, and blacklisting of school districts to secure better salaries and improved working conditions for teachers.

Militancy came earlier in England for the teachers' organizations, and until the 1940s the National Union of Teachers was clearly more effective in protecting teachers than was the National Education Association or the American Federation of Teachers.

The National Union of Teachers (NUT) started in 1870 with a group of elementary school teachers serving children of the lower classes in schools of low status. These teachers were not members of "the establishment" in England (not having gone to private schools and to Oxford or Cambridge) so they had nothing to lose by adopting an attitude of militancy and by forming an informal alliance with labor unions. In contrast, teachers in the United States were desperately eager to achieve middle-class respectability, and for many years defined professional as meaning non-association with working-class people and non-use of such militant tactics as the strike.

In more recent times teachers in England have become middle class and basically conservative. This is especially true of women teachers; they have been characterized as basically opposed to militancy and "unsympathetic to radical postures in dress, manners or political tactics."[3]

In England, as in the United States, there are a host of teachers' organizations dealing with academic fields, such as mathematics; these associations ordinarily don't enter into the struggle for power. In England there are several organizations, in addition to NUT, which do represent the interests of teachers in competition with other groups seeking to control part or all of the educational enterprise. These include the Incorporated Association of Headmasters, the Incorporated Association of Headmistresses, the Association of Assistant Masters, the Association of Assistant Mistresses, the National Association of Head Teachers, and the National Association of Schoolmasters. Except for the latter, and NUT, all of the organizations have small memberships. Those organizations representing the administrators have influence greater than their numbers would suggest, as do the associations for teachers in grammar schools (called assistant masters or mistresses), which are high status institutions attended mainly by middle-class children.

The National Association of Schoolmasters is a militant organization for men teachers only; it was formed to counter what it charges is administrator and female domination in NUT. It prods NUT into greater militancy in a manner very similar to the relationship of the American Federation of Teachers and the National Education Association.

The National Association of Schoolmasters in 1972 enrolled 31 percent of the men teachers and had reached an all-time high of 56,000 members. In 1972 NUT had 31,000 fewer members than the previous year, but its membership still exceeded 300,000. Two-thirds of NUT's membership is female. NUT enrolls less than half of the teachers with a degree. Most of the teachers in England have two or three years of college but no degree; this is true of almost all elementary school teachers, most of the lower secondary school (secondary modern) teachers, and as much as 20 percent of the academic secondary school teachers.

The power of NUT stems from its size, its widespread system of local associations which work to influence local governmental officials and local politicians, and the fact that 25 or so members of Parliament (MP's) receive an annual subsidy (roughly $900) from NUT. This subsidy is a matter of public knowledge and these MP's introduce bills for NUT and generally support legislation favorable to teachers. In 1970 NUT voted to affiliate with the largest labor union group in England, the Trades Union Congress. The expectation was that this would increase the effective pressure that NUT can bring to bear, especially on the national government.

Normally NUT doesn't need to send a formal deputation to the Department of Education and Science on a particular issue because the Department routinely sends NUT a draft of a proposed circular or regulation for comment prior to its being issued. When a deputation is sent it is usually for show—i.e., to remind the public of the issue and to reassure the NUT membership that its leaders are working on the problem.[4] The membership at times needs to be reminded and prodded, in order to overcome a widespread tendency for many members at the local level to be fairly inactive, almost apathetic. Yet the amount of apathy seems no greater than that typically found in trade and professional associations.[5]

At times militant groups within the NUT membership speak out against what they charge is the domination of the organization by administrators (head teachers). They say that these head teachers have allowed the national government to "kick the teachers around."[6] In the top policy-making body, The Executive, five-sixths of the members are head teachers (principals, to use American terminology). In addition, it is charged that oftentimes deals are made quietly by the big boys—i.e., the general secretary of NUT, the executive secretary of the organization representing the Local Education Authorities (Association of Education Committees), and top officials in the Department of Education and Science.[7] Indeed, much of the stability of the relationship between the teachers' organizations and the national government up to 1960, when the national government began to demand more power for itself, was based on the close contact maintained by these top officials, and the good rapport between these men of similar backgrounds.

On occasion NUT has confronted the national government on an issue and taken its case to the people by means of a nationwide campaign of publicity. Such campaigns are infrequent because the NUT leadership has to secure approval beforehand from two-thirds of the membership. In the 1950s there were two such confrontations with the national government. On the matter of changing the system of grants from the national government to the local governments so that there would be no earmarking of funds for schools as distinct from money for roads and other county activities, NUT opposed and lost. Apparently the membership of NUT failed to get as excited about the issue as the leadership. Attempts by the national government to raise the teacher's contribution to the pension fund, on the other hand, aroused a storm of teacher protest, and the matter was dropped after one member of the prime minister's cabinet was forced to resign.[8]

In the 1960s NUT successfully killed the proposed use of semi-professional persons as teacher auxiliaries. Curiously enough, in 1967 NUT mounted a nationwide campaign to relieve teachers of the duties associated with supervision of the noontime meal at school. Two other demands were included, namely that no more unqualified teachers be hired and that the salary scale be changed. NUT threatened to withdraw its teachers from all schools if the three demands were not met.

Beginning in September 1967, NUT carried out its threat by withdrawing teachers from eighteen areas in England. The Secretary of the Department of Education and Science responded by setting up talks between representatives of the teachers and the LEAs. As a result of the negotiations, NUT won on all three points. The supervision of meals duty was lightened as of August 1968, the differential in salary between elementary and secondary school teachers was reduced, and the regulations were changed to specify that no unqualified teachers would be hired after August 31, 1970.[9]

Teachers Lose Power

Militancy on the part of teachers in the 1960s and 1970s in part is due to a growing sense of loss of power. As one official of NUT put it, in 1968, the much publicized partnership (teachers, local governments, and the national government) was a farce. Teachers were not consulted by LEAs or by the national government. The national government made cuts in educational expenditures without consulting the teachers' organizations. He charged further that the advisory boards and ad hoc national commissions usually were not representative of teachers' interests, and the one which was (advisory commission on teacher training and supply) was abolished by the national government when it began to express its views.[10]

Loss of power, or proposed extension of teacher power, come up in a number of areas, such as the following:

a) Comprehensive schools—should teachers be consulted on the question of whether to go comprehensive?
b) Curriculum—was the teacher still king in his own classroom or were other forces at work determining what should be taught and how?
c) Democracy within the school—were teachers to have a say about general policies for their school or were these matters decided entirely by administrators and outside authorities?
d) Membership on board of governors of the school—if this board determined some of the school's policies, should not teachers be on the board, along with the local "establishment" figures usually appointed to the board?
e) Membership on Education Committees of the LEA—should not all LEAs be forced to appoint some teachers to this important arm of the local government?
f) Salaries—teachers' organizations had long played an important part in the negotiating process whereby national salary scales were set, but in the 1960s questions were raised as to whether the national government was assuming an unduly large role in the negotiations.

Comprehensive Schools

By 1964 several LEAs were in the process of reorganizing their secondary school system to merge grammar schools and secondary modern schools to form comprehensive secondary schools. Teachers in the grammar schools were particularly apprehensive about the future of grammar schools, and in January 1964, the Association of Assistant Masters, representing some 27,000 teachers, passed a resolution urging that teachers be consulted before any reorganization occurs.[11] NUT was more favorable to the trend toward comprehensive schools, but throughout the 1960s it also protested about the repeated failure of LEAs to consult the teachers' groups prior to secondary school reorganization.

In some cases teachers were consulted but their position was weakened by differences of opinion among different groups of teachers. Such was the case in Gateshead in the 1964-1967 period as changeover to comprehensive schools was begun. Grammar school teachers—through their organization, The Joint Four—were hostile to the comprehensive school plan, and the local branch of NUT favored it. The views of the grammar school teachers were largely ignored.[12]

In 1969 both of the major political parties endorsed the concept that teachers be consulted prior to the adoption of a new system of secondary education. The Conservative Party linked the concept with a plea that decisions about whether to have comprehensive schools be left to the LEAs, rather than to the national government. The Conservative Party said that if elected it would approve any sound plan from the LEAs which had the backing of parents and teachers.[13]

In many of the LEAs teachers are not consulted about secondary school reorganization as much as teachers would like. And the national government supports or opposes comprehensive schools, depending on which party is in power, without worrying much about what teachers think on the matter.

Control Over Curriculum and Method

It may be that some government officials feel that the teacher should restrict his interests to the classroom where tradition has it, in England anyway, that he is free to follow his professional judgment. The American educator, according to one authority, has far too little of this professional freedom.

> By the very nature of schools, teachers function within a bureaucracy. Bureaucracy means rules and regulations, uniformity, hierarchical relationships. For example, schools must start and stop at a certain time. Courses must have a certain uniformity. Grades, textbooks, credits, and the whole structure of academic bookkeeping impose restrictions that narrow the professional latitude of the individual teacher. No matter how democratically these rules are formulated, once established, no serious deviation is possible. The inevitable result is restriction of the personal freedom of teachers, and this differs from the self-directed course of the physician or lawyer.[14]

To counter the lack of professional freedom, many American teachers' groups have sought and obtained laws forcing local school districts to bargain collectively with the teachers' organizations in the district.

It is widely held that American teachers have relatively little power over many things that affect the quality of the teaching that goes on in the classroom.[15] American educators, on the other hand, in discussing schools in England tend to exaggerate the independence exercised by English teachers. The following quote is typical of this exaggerated view:

> English classroom teachers determine their own instructional programs; they are the ones who make the ultimate decisions about what they have been hired to do with children.[16]

In fact, teachers in England tend to dissipate whatever power they might have by dividing along the usual lines of age, sex, marital status, and whether they favor progressive or traditional approaches. They also differ in their "degree of support for or apathy toward the head [administrator]."[17]

It is the head teacher or headmaster who really has control over curriculum rather than the classroom teacher, and

American observers cloud the issue by exaggerating the amount of part-time teaching done by this official and underplaying the fact that he is an administrator with considerable power. The administrator tends to set the tone of the school with regard to curriculum and method, and a conservative teacher finds it difficult to work in a progressive school, and vice versa for the progressive teacher in a conservative school.[18]

The individual school in England (chiefly via its headmaster) does have considerable autonomy compared to a particular school in the United States, and this lack of school autonomy has been cited as a major factor in the failure of curriculum reform in the United States. Curriculum changes in the United States are imposed on teachers and then the teachers are taught how to function in the new situation. Teachers' organizations have done little to protect American teachers from this imposition.[19]

Englishmen differ on how much credence they give to the proposition that the teacher in England is the judge of what he shall teach and how he shall teach. Typical of those on the optimistic side is retired chief inspector (HMI) John Blackie, who argued in 1969 that the elementary school teacher in England was freer than his counterpart anywhere else in the world.[20] On the other side is an English educator's pessimistic comment, in 1972, about the secondary school:

> The processes by which the English school curriculum is controlled are devious in the extreme. Over much of the secondary curriculum they take the form of a grand theoretical freedom for the teachers to plan their own courses and a practical strait jacket imposed by an external examination in league with a tough system of university selection.[21]

According to one English educator,[22] teachers are losing control over the curriculum, and it is occurring in subtle ways. In fact, he says, the independence of the teacher in England never was as great as the official ideology would have it. Most teachers received considerable direction from the head teacher—except in certain grammar schools where the headmaster felt that it was unprofessional to interfere. Yet, teachers (especially the strong-willed ones) had a measure of freedom which would surprise a teacher in France.

All that is threatened now by developments which call for coordination and cooperation and adherence to a centralized plan. For example, with the new media, TV and programmed learning, every teacher has to pretty much stick to the schedule, and those who design the programs are in control—not the individual teacher. It has even been suggested that the much publicized open education and integrated curriculum may amount to a diminution of the power of the teacher, who now becomes an interchangable part rather than a master of a particular subject or classroom.

> Integrated curricula are powerless curricula, wide open to centralized control. They present no effective curb on the will of the man at the top.[23]

The Schools Council has encouraged teachers to come together to share ideas. In itself sharing is a good thing, but it ends up with a higher degree of uniformity, and teachers are no longer choosing their own materials and approaches to teaching. In fact, the three-year report in 1967 from the Schools Council indicated that the Council saw its role as that of moving the teachers toward new approaches and materials—i.e., toward "reform."[24]

Those who are enthusiastic about the work of the Schools Council and the centers where teachers gather to discuss curriculum see them as ways in which teachers can have a significant voice in determining curriculum and method reforms. It is even suggested that teachers now have an opportunity to work systematically on curriculum reform instead of relying on innovations imported from the United

States.[25] One observer, however, claims that so far very few curriculum changes have come from the classroom teachers. Instead, there is a growing trend of teachers relying on packaged materials distributed by commercial firms.[26]

Teachers in England are not used to working on formal projects and often seem to be uncertain as to how to proceed. Then, too, notices of proposed teacher-run projects have to be channeled through the headmaster of each school and the word doesn't always get to the teachers. In fact, many headmasters and head teachers may not appreciate the importance of teacher involvement in curriculum change. An important exception may be the heads of nursery schools and the heads of open or progressive elementary schools.

Teacher participation on curriculum projects sometimes gets sidetracked by such political issues as the amount of representation the various teachers' groups will have on the Schools Council. It has been pointed out that the work of the teacher centers and the curriculum projects of the Schools Council represent a unique opportunity and if wasted "then the autonomy of the teacher will become a myth or legend of the past."[27]

During the last 100 years in England the autonomy of the teacher apparently fluctuated depending on whether it was a time of liberal movements or one of reaction. For example, reduction of the teacher's freedom occurred in the "payment by results" period (1861 to the 1890s) when the teacher's pay was determined by his pupils' scores on tests given by the national inspectors (HMIs), and again in the late 1960s and 1970s when a reaction set in against the open or free classrooms and the permissiveness that was associated with these progressive approaches.

During the reaction periods there is a tendency to introduce cost accounting and other "efficiency" measures as society steps in to make certain that it gets its money's worth.[28]

During the liberal periods interest centers on the child, and teachers are encouraged to exercise initiative in devising challenging and interesting ways for children to learn and to grow.[29] The open classroom movement in England's elementary schools in the 1960s and 1970s and the "free schools" and American counterparts of the open classroom approach would be examples.

The "ban the cane" movement in England in the 1970s illustrates how liberal movements and reaction are closely related and the effects on teacher autonomy. The "cane" is a code word for whipping children, which still occurs in some English schools. As certain LEAs began to issue directives "banning the cane," teachers' groups reacted angrily.

NUT, the National Association of Schoolmasters, and especially the National Association of Headteachers, opposed any interference from citizens or politicians on the matter of disciplining pupils. The teachers were not just objecting to the threatened loss of a professional's right to choose his own way of managing children. The teachers linked the "ban the cane" movement to the "violence in the classroom" issue, which was a matter of growing concern. In 1972, a research study (sponsored by the National Association of Schoolmasters) on pupil violence reported that in the first half of that school year there were 983 reported cases of primary school pupils attacking each other or a teacher with a weapon, such as a knife, and 3200 such cases in secondary schools among pupils in the 11-16 age range.[30] The National Association of Schoolmasters then warned that it would have a direct confrontation with any LEA which refused a headmaster the power to suspend a troublesome pupil.[31]

Not all of the teachers agreed on the need to whip children. The young teachers in London have formed a separate teachers' organization, which came out with the recommendation that the way to end violence in the classroom was not to retain the cane but rather to end the "prison" atmosphere in most schools. To that end it recommended the inclusion of pupils, parents, and teachers in decision making. The suggestion reflected a growing demand for democratic participation in society's institutions, including the schools.

Democracy in the Schools

Teachers in England, compared to industrial workers, have been slow to demand a say-so on school-wide matters. In part this may have been because they had considerable freedom to run their own classrooms and settled for that.[32]

The need for greater teacher participation in policy making was articulated in 1963 by John Vaizey in his book *The Control of Education:*

> ... as a matter of urgency the teachers have the task ahead of them of seeking professional status; and of seeking a role in educational policy-making which is greater than that they play at present.[33]

The same point was being made in the United States, and in 1966 leaders of both the National Education Association and the American Federation of Teachers militantly asserted that teachers must be involved more in policy making.[34]

American school administrators in recent years have been encouraged to involve teachers more in decisions. The rationale for this is usually improvement of teacher morale rather than a desire to share power with teachers.[35] This new emphasis on "democratic administration" is an outgrowth of the human relations movement. Usually the administrators favor teacher participation up to a point. Typically the administrator falls back on the principle that final decisions rest with the administrator.[36]

In the United States demands by teachers for involvement in policy making undoubtedly have been stimulated by government regulations which require that poor people be involved in policy making in "war on poverty" programs and parents be involved in policy making in "Headstart" and similar early childhood projects. Then, too, the consolidation of small districts into large ones tends to dwarf the individual teacher and increase his resistance to "the system," unless he has a hand in making the rules.[37] In addition, teachers are better educated now, more confident, and feel that they should participate in policy decisions.

Teachers in England also are better educated now. Those trained in the 1960s and 1970s in the colleges of education have had three years of college instead of two, and a small group complete a fourth year and receive a degree. Also, teachers in England are inbibing at the same spring of grass-roots democracy as American teachers.

The Plowden Report in 1967 called for more participation by teachers in the governing of their school. The actual language was a bit cautious, namely that "staff should be drawn as much as possible into the planning and organisation of school life."[38]

In 1969, two professors at the University of Bradford made a study of teachers' attitudes. They found that teachers wanted more say in the making of educational policy. They did not want the headmaster's power to increase, and they hoped to see a reduction in county educational officials' control over educational policy.[39]

At the end of the 1960s NUT took note of a trend to include teachers on governing boards, especially in colleges of education and technical institutions. Some elementary and secondary schools were establishing staff councils, and NUT expressed the hope that all schools would establish such a body and give it a role to play in policy making.[40]

At the annual conference of NUT in 1969 a group of young teachers formed a militant bloc and suggested a campaign to include teachers in the running of the school. They called for "clearly defined democratic powers in the making and carrying out of policy within the schools." Teachers should have a say on curriculum and teaching methods, on matters of discipline, and on how the schools funds were spent. In addition, there should be the "highest degree of involvement" in the hiring of new staff and in writing letters of recommendation for those staff members leaving the school. It was even recommended that all correspondence to the school be seen by all the staff, though there were dissenters on this point. Finally, harsh words were directed toward the school's administrator, called principal in the U.S. and "head," head teacher, or headmaster in England.

> The position of the head is an autocratic one. It is difficult for a head not to be an autocrat. And an assistant teacher [England's name for a regular teacher] is entirely at the mercy of his head.[41]

It was inevitable that demands for extension of the teachers' control over internal policy for the school would run up against the vested interests of the administrator—the head teacher. What England's teachers have to contend with is the remnants of a tradition of strong headmasters, especially the strong leader model set by famous nineteenth century private school headmasters.

Conflict broke out into the open in 1969 over the issue of whether the head teachers could order their teachers to supervise the noon meal at school or whether teachers were within their professional rights to refuse such duty. Both sides claim that the law is on their side, and strikes over these kinds of issues continue to erupt in various LEAs.

In 1971 a resolution was passed at the annual meeting of NUT to check into means of establishing better consultation between teachers and the head teachers and to redefine the role of the head teacher. NUT then set up a series of regional meetings to discuss the issue of more teacher participation in policy making, including the possibility of establishing councils in each school made up of elected teacher representatives to make policy on curriculum, school reorganization, internal school finance and parent-teacher relations. The head teacher was to be on ex officio member of the council.[42] The *Times Educational Supplement* reacted to the proposal by editorializing that much quiet sharing of power with teachers was occurring in many LEAs and asked whether goodwill would come from any forcing of the issue.[43]

In the United States sentiment for forcing the issue increased as bureaucratization of the school enterprise made it less likely that an individual teacher would have much chance of being listened to by those in power.

> Irreversible changes in the structure of public education requires, in short, that the bureaucratic strength of the administrator be matched by the organizational strength of the teachers.[44]

In the United States the issue was forced as various state teachers' organizations secured the passage of state laws forcing each school district to engage in formal bargaining sessions with the teachers' organization in the district to determine salaries, working conditions and other matters. By 1971 approximately 70 percent of the public school teachers in the United States were covered by collective negotiation procedures.

Curiously, these collective bargaining procedures have enhanced the powers of the chief administrator—i.e., the superintendent of the county, or city, school system. This occurs because the school board must give its representative at the bargaining sessions (the superintendent) considerable freedom to maneuver if he is to perform his role effectively. At the same time the teachers' organizations have acquired more political strength as their staffs have expanded to participate in the bargaining sessions. When the bargaining sessions are over these staff persons are then free to engage in lobbying activities with the state legislature.[45]

Teacher Representation

Bargaining with the individual LEAs was not a possibility for NUT, but within the English context there were other ways to ensure greater teacher participation in policy making. Some of these ways were cited in 1970 and 1971 as resolutions were passed at the annual conference of NUT calling on the leadership of the Union to mount a campaign to secure laws or directives from the national government requiring all LEAs to provide:[46]

1. teacher representation on the Education Committee of the LEA;
2. teacher representation on the board of governors, which every school in England must have if it receives public tax money;
3. machinery in every school for teachers to participate in policy decisions on curriculum and other matters.

The need for more teacher representation on these policy-making bodies had been spelled out in the early 1960s by John Vaizey, economist and a leading spokesman on educational matters for the Labor Party. Speaking on the issue of salaries he suggested that the old-fashioned tactics of pressure were not effective and teachers' organizations would do better to imitate the medical profession and secure greater representation of teachers on all the key policy-making bodies. Then better salaries would follow as a matter of course.[47]

The Plowden Report said that teachers should have access to the board of managers of a school and to officials of the LEA; the implication was that they did not have such access. The Plowden Report also recommended that teachers should be appointed to the Education Committee of the LEA.[48]

By the late 1960s only a few LEAs had failed to appoint at least one teacher to the Education Committee, which handled most of the education work of the LEA. In 1968 the head of the Department of Education and Science sent a circular letter to all LEAs urging them to add teachers to their Education Committees. NUT applauded this applying of pressure by the national government.[49]

In the same year, 1969, the Association of Education Committees came out in favor of a law to require that teachers be represented on all Education Committees in all LEAs.[50] NUT also called for a law requiring "substantial numbers" of teacher representatives on Education Committees. As NUT put it, schools, in their methods and organization, had become too complex for lay people to understand fully, and teachers could be very useful on Education Committees if given full voting privileges. NUT claimed that teachers on Education Committees frequently were excluded from important subcommittees on the grounds of conflict of interest. NUT also suggested that the lay persons on the Education Committee be interested and informed on education and that they be nominated by "recognized educational interests in the locality"[51] —meaning teachers' organizations.

NUT also called for legal requirements that teachers be represented on all boards of governors, or boards of managers as they are called in the case of elementary schools. This idea was supported by the Association of Assistant Masters.

Teachers also became sensitive to proper teacher representation on important national ad hoc committees. Thus, in 1972 there was criticism of the newly appointed committee to study "reading and the use of English" because no classroom teachers were included. The reply of the Department of Education and Science was that there were school administrators (head teachers) on the committee and that they had considerable classroom experience.[52] Such a reply was notably out of step with the prevailing views of teachers and seemed likely to add fuel to a growing mood of militancy among teachers.

Militancy

Militancy in teachers in both England and the United States was a factor to be reckoned with from the 1960s onward. In the case of American teachers, the militancy seems to be an outgrowth of the following factors:[53]

1. Increasing bureaucratization and centralization isolate teachers from the decision-making process.

2. Educational bureaucracies are not working well—not coping with the problems—so teachers don't respect or accept the authority of administrators.

3. There is insufficient opportunity for movement upward in teaching and ambitious teachers are left with a feeling of frustration, which can lead to anger.

4. Teachers are increasingly aware that their work is shaped by outside forces and groups beyond their control.

5. Low salaries and poor working conditions have become intolerable, especially in city school systems.

6. Teachers have command of new specialities, such as the new math or the Initial Teaching Alphabet, which administrators can't challenge.

7. At the same time the lack of teacher participation in decision making is out of step with the times and angers teachers.

8. The size of the teaching force is getting larger, and teachers are no longer dispersed but rather are found in and around urban centers. Cities seem to spawn friction and aggressive behavior.

9. The climate of the times favors militancy thanks to the Civil Rights movement, the ending of colonialism, and a general rejection of paternalism.

10. More men have entered the teaching profession; men teachers have the reputation of being more militant than women teachers.

Teacher militancy in both England and the United States can also be viewed as an attempt to counter what in the United States is called the "accountability" movement. The accountability movement reflects a growing trend to break everything in our society down into measurable units which can be handled in a very precise, and presumably scientific, way. For the teacher this involves an elaborate attempt to break his endeavors down into parts and then to check on how the teacher performs every step of his work. Finally it attempts to measure the product of this educational effort, namely the student and how he performs on specific tasks.

Accountability procedures reportedly work well in automobile factories and result in ever higher numbers of automobiles produced each year. The procedures sometimes include a supervisor standing at a worker's side with a stopwatch to see that he works steadily and with a minimum of wasted motion. Such close supervision is anathema to professionals.

American teachers, through their organizations, have fought back by demanding contracts which spell out in great detail what a teacher will be required to do, and by implication what he will not be required to do. Some in the profession have wondered whether the effect of such contracts is to restrict professional autonomy and discourage professional attitudes in teachers.

> Could it not be argued that the more detailed the contract the more the agreement is sprayed with minutiae, the farther removed from "professional" everybody gets. For, by virtue of the spelling out of detail, general principles are defined and, thus, restricted. This very restriction cramps professional style and flexibility.[54]

Recently in England teachers have taken to acting like unskilled workers as a way of saying if you don't treat us as professionals we won't act as professionals. One of the tactics is called "working-to-rule;" in other words, teachers will perform those duties specified by law or by government directives and no others. Thus, supervising student clubs after school is refused since it is not included in the rules. As the *Times Educational Supplement* put it in 1969, in referring to teachers, "Strike action, work-to-rule, and impatience with authority are no longer the preserve of either students or manual workers."[55]

Militancy was put to the vote of the NUT membership and showed increasing strength. In February 1969, at a special conference to discuss the problem of adequate salaries, the resolution for militant tactics received 90,791 votes to 134,833 against.[56]

At NUT's annual conference in April 1969, the militants pressed for the creation of a strike fund by a levy of £1 per year on each member, and they forced through resolutions ordering the Union leadership to demand of the national government that the salary scale be nenegotiated. The Union leadership, officers and the executive, opposed the resolutions.[57] Leadership of NUT has long been composed overwhelmingly of male administrators (head teachers, headmasters, and chief education officers of LEAs).

In the same year the National Association of Schoolmasters (NAS) also used the "work-to-rule" tactic in individual LEAs to force the national government to reopen the salary question. In some of the LEAs teachers engaging in "work-to-rule" were fired, and NAS retaliated by calling all its teachers out on strike. Durham was one such area, even though it was a working-class community dominated by the Labor Party. The strike by NAS teachers dragged on for fourteen weeks. The same thing happened in London as NAS teachers "worked-to-rule" by refusing to teach in classes with more than thirty pupils, since the rule specified thirty as a maximum. In 1972 in Teeside, some 850 teachers worked-to-rule for several months and eventually 156 teachers were placed under suspension as NAS threatened counteractions.[58]

The militancy of the National Association of Schoolmasters paid off in a dramatic rise of membership exceeding 10,000 new members per year in the 1970s, just as militancy by the American Federation of Teachers in the United States increased the membership of that organization. NAS membership in 1971 was over 50,000, compared to 21,000 ten years earlier.

NUT got the message, and in the fall of 1969 leaders in the organization announced that "teachers are fed up and are now ready to fight for what they want and need."[59] Such fighting words reflected the competition of NAS, but also the presence within NUT of a large bloc of young militant teachers. The Young Teachers group was reported to be 100,000 strong, and they met separately and called for a one-day nationwide strike of teachers to dramatize the salary issue.[60]

At the annual conference of NUT in the spring of 1970 the "moderates" prevailed, but by this time all elements in the Union were for some degree of militancy. NUT voted to pick selected areas of England that fall to strike if class size exceeded the rule (thirty pupils for secondary schools and forty for elementary schools).[61]

Strikes by teachers have become commonplace in the United States also. The opening of school in 1972 was marked by teacher strikes in Pennsylvania, Rhode Island, Missouri, Illinois and a number of other states. In Pennsylvania alone, some 350,000 students were unable to attend school in twenty school districts where teachers were out on strike.[62] Philadelphia teachers, who were out on strike in the fall of 1972 for three weeks, went out on strike again in January 1973; close to 300,000 pupils in Philadelphia were out of school. At the same time, January 1973, Chicago's teachers went out on strike for the third time in four years; the Chicago public schools have approximately 26,000 teachers and over half-a-million students. Teachers in St. Louis also went on strike in January 1973.

Militancy is now an accepted part of the educational scene in England and in the United States.

NOTES

1. Jules Henry, "Is Education Possible?" p. 117 in C. A. Bowers, Ian Housego and Doris Dyke, eds., *Education and Social Policy: Local Control of Education.* New York: Random House, 1970.
2. Frank Musgrove and Philip H. Taylor, *Society and the Teacher's Role.* London: Routledge and Kegan Paul, 1969, p. 82.
3. Robert J. Fisher, *Learning How to Learn: The English Primary School and American Education.* New York: Harcourt, Brace and Jovanovich, 1972, p. 67.
4. Ronald A. Manzer, *Teachers and Politics in England and Wales.* Toronto, Can.: Univ. of Toronto Press, 1970, p. 11.
5. The lack of participation by all but a dedicated few in NUT is discussed in Walter Roy, *The Teacher's Union: Aspects of Policy and*

Organization in the National Union of Teachers, 1950-1966. London: Schoolmaster Pub. Co., 1968, pp. 1-56.

6. Ibid., p. 74.
7. Manzer, op. cit., pp. 8-10.
8. Ibid., p. 146.
9. Ibid., p. 14.
10. Times Educational Supplement (London), February 2, 1968, p. 356.
11. Ibid., January 3, 1964, p. 13.
12. Richard Batley, Oswald O'Brien, and Henry Parris, *Going Comprehensive: Educational Policy-Making in Two County Boroughs.* London: Routledge and Kegan Paul, 1970, pp. 67, 81-83.
13. Times Educational Supplement (London), September 12, 1969, p. 28.
14. Sol Elkins, "Another Look at Collective Negotiations for Professionals," School and Society, Vol. 98, No. 2324, March 1970, p. 173.
15. For example, see Seymour B. Sarason, *The Culture of the School and the Problem of Change.* Boston: Allyn and Bacon, 1971, p. 154.
16. Fisher, op. cit., p. 7.
17. Ibid., p. 67.
18. Maurice Kogan, *The Government of Education.* New York: Citation, 1971, p. 30.
19. Fisher, op. cit., pp. 21, 26.
20. John Blackie, "The Character and Aims of British Primary Education," pp. 1-5 in Geoffrey Howson, ed., *Children At School: Primary Education in Britain Today.* New York: Teachers College Press, 1969.
21. Times Educational Supplement (London), June 16, 1972, p. 1.
22. David Wardle, *English Popular Education, 1780-1970.* London: Cambridge Univ. Press, 1970, pp. 155-156.
23. Frank Musgrove, *Patterns of Power and Authority in English Education.* London: Methuen, 1971, p. 7.
24. Wardle, op. cit., pp. 155-156.
25. Elizabeth Adams, "Teachers, Research and Curriculum Development," p. 187 in Edmund J. King, ed., *The Teacher and the Needs of Society in Evolution.* New York: Pergamon, 1970.
26. Fisher, op. cit., pp. 18, 151.
27. Adams, op. cit., p. 187.
28. Wardle, op. cit., pp. 161-162. For a good historical treatment of the efficiency movement in American education, see Raymond E. Callahan, *Education and the Cult of Efficiency.* Chicago: Univ. of Chicago Press, 1962.

29. Wardle, op. cit., pp. 161-162.
30. Times Educational Supplement (London), June 30, 1972, p. 5.
31. Ibid., July 14, 1972, p. 5.
32. Musgrove, op. cit., p. 69.
33. John Vaizey, *The Control of Education*. London: Faber and Faber, 1963, p. 223.
34. Alan Rosenthal, ed., *Governing Education: A Reader on Politics, Power, and Public School Policy*. Garden City, N.Y.: Anchor, 1969, pp. 291-292.
35. Frederick M. Wirt and Michael W. Kirst, *The Political Web of American Schools*. Boston: Little, Brown, 1972, pp. 50-51.
36. Alan Rosenthal, *Pedagogues and Power: Teacher Groups in School Politics*. Syracuse, N.Y.: Syracuse Univ. Press, 1969, pp. 3-5.
37. Henry Ehlers, ed., *Crucial Issues in Education*, fourth ed. New York: Rinehart and Winston, 1969, pp. 312-314.
38. Central Advisory Council for Education (England). *Children and their Primary Schools*, Vol. I. London: Her Majesty's Stationery Office, 1967, p. 418.
39. Times Educational Supplement (London), April 4, 1969, p. 1095.
40. National Union of Teachers. *Into the 70's*. London: NUT, 1969, p. 26.
41. Times Educational Supplement (London), September 19, 1969, p. 12.
42. Ibid., July 16, 1971, p. 3.
43. Ibid.
44. Rosenthal, *Pedagogues and Power*, op. cit., pp. 13-14.
45. Myron Lieberman, "The Future of Collective Negotiations." Phi Delta Kappan, Vol. LIII, No. 4, Dec. 1971, p. 215.
46. National Union of Teachers of England and Wales. *Teacher Participation: A Study Outline*. London: NUT, 1971, p. 12.
47. John Vaizey, *Britain in the Sixties: Education for Tomorrow*. London: Penguin, 1962, pp. 92-97.
48. *Children and their Primary Schools*, op. cit., pp. 413, 420.
49. Times Educational Supplement (London), August 23, 1968, p. 320.
50. Ibid., March 21, 1969, p. 928.
51. *Into the 70's*, op. cit., pp. 24-25.
52. Ibid., July 2, 1972, p. 10.
53. See Seymour B. Sarason, op. cit., p. 154; Rosenthal, *Pedagogues and Power*, op. cit., pp. 13-15; Ronald G. Corwin, "Teacher Militancy in the United States: Reflections on its Sources and Prospects," pp. 291-300 in Harold Full, ed., *Controversies in American Education:*

An Anthology of Crucial Issues, second ed. New York: MacMillan, 1972.

54. Lester S. Vander Werf, "Militancy and the Profession of Teaching." School and Society, Vol. 98, No. 2324, March 1970, pp. 171-173.

55. Times Educational Supplement (London), February 21, 1969, p. 571.

56. Ibid.

57. Ibid., April 4, 1969, p. 1093 and April 11, 1969, p. 1170.

58. Ibid., December 22, 1972, p. 3.

59. Ibid., October 17, 1969, p. 9.

60. Ibid., September 19, 1969, p. 12.

61. Ibid., April 3, 1970, p. 1.

62. Washington Post, September 8, 1972, p. A-14. For a description of the outbreak of teachers' strikes in the 1960s, see Rosenthal, *Pedagogues and Power,* op. cit., pp. 17-19.

Chapter 5

THE BOSSES—EROSION OF AUTHORITY

As one leaves the level of the classroom teacher in England and moves up through the hierarchy of power he encounters the headmaster (or head teacher), the board of governors (each school has one), and the chief education officer of the Local Education Authority (LEA). Beyond all this lies the local government, functioning mostly through its Education Committee, and the national government. The chief education officer, though an employee of the LEA, is an educator and will be discussed in this chapter, along with the headmaster and the board of governors.

Headmaster

The tradition of strong headmasters dates back to at least the nineteenth century.[1] During that century, when schools became large enough one man was singled out as the head teacher. After a while such men were rewarded for their organizational skill and ability to lead (and control) employees. The headmaster often acquired the de facto power to hire and fire teachers.[2]

The early headmasters often were men of social and academic standing, and they were able to reduce the amount of interference by the school's board of governors;[3] the tradition of headmaster autonomy thus established has stood the modern headmaster in good stead as he deals with his board of governors, or even with the chief education officers of the LEA. It should be noted, however, that this tradition applies more to secondary school headmasters than to elementary school heads and that the original nineteenth century model was a private school—one not obligated to serve the public, then or now.

In the twentieth century the state-supported secondary schools copied the private school model as best they could. They were seldom able, however, to match the private school headmaster's skillful use of older pupils and an arsenal of physical and psychological punishments, to keep the student body in line.

By the 1920s in the state-supported schools, the headmaster's powers were curtailed some as teachers began to acquire tenure and as the whole country moved away from the heavy-handed leadership so characteristic of Victorian authoritarianism.[4] Moreover, the slow but steady bureaucratization of the school system—whereby orderly procedures for hiring, firing and promoting teachers were instituted—meant that the teachers were less subject to capricious whim of a particular headmaster.[5]

The second half of the twentieth century saw further erosion of the headmaster's powers. The headmasters, particularly in the academic secondary schools (grammar schools), experienced some loss of their autonomy after World War II as the LEAs and the national government tightened up the administration of schools as part of a program to make them more efficient and more responsive to national needs.

The stature of heads was diminished by a few inches when they began to receive circular letters from the Education Office (Chief Education Officer of the LEA) impersonally addressed to "The Head Teacher." In time they grew accustomed to the lower altitude, but their resentment at having to fill in forms in triplicate or ask official permission for the use of their own classrooms for out-of-school activities was not all caused rationally by the considerable amount of extra routine work which these activities entailed. They also felt, and were correct in feeling, that however necessary such measures might seem to be in the interests of the greatest happiness of the greatest number, the autonomy of their own schools was seriously threatened.[6]

Some bureaucratic regulations were an outgrowth of the Education Act of 1944, which called for more coordination and supervision of schools, especially by the national government. Some of the accretion of rules and regulations was a natural accompaniment of growing size, and some reflected the slow growth in stature of the post of chief education officer in the LEA.

Nonetheless, as of 1960 the headmaster typically was still a powerful figure with considerable control over curriculum, teaching methods, and the like. One English educator, in 1961, contended that the English headmaster had more power than his counterpart in most other countries.[7] Often such statements had in mind the headmasters of the famous private schools; as late as the mid 1960s these men were described as wielding immense power and as being "insulated against the outside world."[8]

Those who compare the headmaster or head teacher of England's tax-supported schools with the principal in an American school tend to emphasize the autonomy of the English administrator compared to his American counterpart. The American principal is seen as trying to pacify parents with public relations techniques while getting teachers to obey rules set by higher educational authorities—namely the school board and the superintendent of schools. The English head teacher is less responsive to public pressure, with the possible exception of the progressive schools ("open schools") which deliberately seek to increase parental involvement.[9]

In England it is difficult for parents to bring pressure to bear on the head teacher or headmaster, even in the case of an incompetent ("less able") one. This also means that it is difficult to enforce a national policy of education.[10] Perhaps this is one reason why the national government is so aggressively looking for ways to extend its powers over the educational enterprise.

The American principal is to some extent a prisoner of a myth that the system prevents him from exercising power. The fact that some principals exercise considerable initiative suggests that some of the limitations on the principal are self-imposed.[11] In contrast, the English head teacher lives with a myth that he still has considerable power and at times acts like a despot. Reportedly, however, he is a despot over trivial things; the important matters—including discretion for himself and his teachers to attend conferences, meetings, and the like—are decided by others.

> But headmasters are petty despots. They are not despots on the grand scale because they have no voice in the major issues which concern their schools.[12]

Whether or not a headmaster, in either private or county schools, chooses to share his powers with his teachers depends on the situation and the personality of the man. In many situations the headmaster's power is tempered by the need to associate closely with his teachers.

> Inside the school, the head may share his responsibility as much or as little as he wishes: as far as governors or Education Committees are concerned, he is the responsible person and this is the source of his power. Even in what appears to be the most autocratically run institutions, however, the subtle interplay of personalities and the coming into existence of conventions and traditions may produce fascinating modifications in this simple

structure of authority. Headmasters, indeed, are not what they were: the day of the great headmaster, that awe-inspiring figure whose word was law and who could look into your very soul, has gone-forever, one hopes.[13]

It is not common in English schools to find administrators ordering teachers around.

There is no need to issue directives or enforce administrative decisions or distribute policy statements through the chain of command... Authorities seldom resort to coercion; it is usually sufficient to carefully make their wishes known.[14]

Whether teachers are more free or less free in a low-key atmosphere where custom and tradition reign is a open question.

English schools are small, intimate places by American standards (the elementary school in England often has under 300 children and the grammar school 700 or so). Even the comprehensive schools seldom exceed 2000 students.

The comprehensive schools of 1000 or more students are big institutions to the English, and in recent years the growth of these institutions has altered the role of the headmaster. In such institutions there is a tendency to delegate authority to lesser administrators and to develop more formal lines of communication. This contrasts sharply with the image at the beginning of the 1960s where the headmaster had little or no formal training in administration and significantly called his quarters in his school a "study" rather than an "office." As one American observer said, after a year-long stay in England, "the American principal views himself as an executive and an administrator, while the headmaster of an English school sees himself as a head teacher."[15]

The teachers in England are not surprised to get suggestions on curriculum and methods from the head teacher. In contrast, the American principal who seeks to please everybody—parents, teachers, superintendent and school board—often finds it convenient not to tamper with the status quo as regards curriculum and method, thus giving teachers a measure of freedom in a negative way.

By the second half of the 1960s the powers of the head teacher had been reduced noticeably, as was noted by the Plowden Report: "There is a good deal of evidence that heads are sometimes ignored or by-passed by authorities where they clearly ought to have a say."[16]

The Plowden Report asserted specifically that:

a) on major or minor repairs to the school the head teacher (and his staff) should be consulted;
b) the head teacher should have some control over the use of his school in out-of-school hours, or at the least be informed of the use being made of the building;
c) head teachers should have a fund to purchase small items for the school;
d) it should be up to the discretion of the head teacher as to when he or any of his staff need to be absent from the school building.[17]

The Plowden Report also recommended "that the head teachers should be consulted by the authority (LEA) on staff appointments so that, wherever possible, marked deficiencies in a staff can be made good."[18]

Events of the 1960s and 1970s have undermined the administrator's position. For one thing, in many LEAs the headmaster of a particular school no longer has the right to select which children he will admit to his school. Children are assigned by the LEA in such a way as to achieve a balance of working-class and middle-class children. In many communities parents are demanding a say in things, and when put off by a particular headmaster they are not above protesting to the national government.

The LEA itself sometimes brings pressure to bear on the headmaster by way of suggestions from local inspectors and the chief education officer which have the effect of pressuring for certain changes. Thus, the prevailing style of education in the LEA sets limits for the headmaster.[19]

Advances in the various fields of knowledge and the changing nature of the elementary school curriculum have made it difficult for the administrator to pretend to be fully in command of the situation. The American principal has to contend with an increasing number of specialists who visit his school for brief periods of time and not only have command of esoteric knowledge and techniques beyond the principal's grasp, but also are not part of his regular staff and not fully subject to his control.[20] The English head teacher has had to lean increasingly on the expertise of his teachers, and the Plowden Report encouraged this sharing of responsibility with teachers.

> In the past head teachers were responsible for all schemes of work. Now that the primary school curriculum is being widened, it is increasingly difficult for them to be up to date with all the developments and sensible that they should invite the help of assistant teachers [England's name for regular teachers] in preparing schemes, in giving advice to their colleagues and in the selection of books, materials and equipment.[21]

Teachers, in fact, are demanding a say in things, often at the expense of the headmaster. By the end of the 1960s teachers in various LEAs were challenging the right of the headmaster to assign them to non-teaching duties, such as supervision of the lunch period at school. NUT was under great pressure from militant members, especially the young teachers (some 100,000 strong) to support teachers who refused to obey the headmaster. Where teachers were fired for failing to obey the headmaster, units of NUT and the National Association of Schoolmasters went out on strike.

The heads reacted to teacher pressure by reasserting their powers and demanding a strengthening of such powers. In 1969 the Association of Head Teachers declared that:

> ... insufficient authority is delegated to the head teacher in the appointment of assistant teachers. Head teachers should be able to appoint assistant teachers with help or guidance as required

from the Chief Education Officer and the chairman of the schools governors, or their representative.[22]

In a conference that same year a group of head teachers (from elementary and secondary schools) asserted that head teachers must have absolute authority in running their schools. It was agreed, however, that the heads should canvas teachers' opinions regularly and be willing to tolerate criticism.[23]

The 1970 annual conference of the Headmasters' Association (which now included 500 heads from comprehensive schools out of the Association's 1800 menbers) took as its main theme the changing authority of the headmaster.[24]

At times NUT supported a head teacher when the opponent was the national government or one of the LEAs. This was the case in 1971 when the headmistress of an elementary school refused to accept fourteen extra children assigned to what she claimed was an already overcrowded school. When the Education Committee of the LEA suspended her, her teachers went out on strike for a week while NUT and the Education Committee negotiated. The Education Committee tried to placate the teachers by shifting the blame to the national government for failing two years earlier to approve the LEA's request for new elementary school facilities.[25]

At this point NUT had already locked horns with the national government over what NUT charged was an attempt to shift control over curriculum from the headmaster to the board of governors of each school. In 1971 this had come up as an issue in two areas (Huntingdon and Peterborough) which sought national government approval of the articles of government for new comprehensive schools. The Department of Education and Science delayed approval of these documents and, as NUT saw it, was trying to give additional control over curriculum to the board of governors.

The Department of Education and Science may have been responding to criticism that the results of educational research were not picked up readily and adapted to classroom practice.[26] It was even suggested that on curriculum matters the supposedly powerful headmaster was limited by public opinion,[27] and by what was in vogue. In some cases LEAs specifically prohibited the teaching of certain materials. This was the case in Birmingham in 1971 when the Education Committee of the LEA ordered all headmasters not to allow the showing of a sex education film titled "Growing Up." The action was upheld by the Birmingham City Council by a vote of 66 to 4.[28]

In the 1970s the National Association of Schoolmasters took the lead in pressing for specific "contracts of service" spelling out such things as class size, leaves of absence for teachers, free periods during the day, restrictions on the use of confidential reports on teachers, and so on.[29] As such matters are spelled out in legal documents they leave little room to maneuver for headmasters and LEA officials.

Headmasters and head teachers are also influenced subtly by the politics of the particular LEA where they work. Thus, it turns out that heads are usually of the same political party dominant in the county. There is little evidence to suggest that the political party tries to dictate to the headmaster but rather that there is a similarity of viewpoint.[30] Such has long been the case with the famous private schools where the headmaster tends to have a background similar to that of the parents. Thus, a study in the 1960s of 84 of the famous private schools showed that 43 percent of the headmasters had attended Oxford University and 52 percent Cambridge.[31]

Headmasters and head teachers in the state-supported school now face the prospect of serving under larger LEAs when the report of a national commission (Maud Report) is implemented in the mid-1970s. Some experts claim that as the 145 smaller LEAs are replaced by larger ones (numbering about 90) the power of the headmaster will be enhanced. The theory, presumably, is that in larger units of bureaucracy the individual school may escape close scrutiny. Yet there is the other possibility that larger size generates rules and regulations of the same kind which began to erode the traditional autonomy of the headmaster after World War II. It might even begin the process of reshaping the headmaster in the image of the American school administrator.

Thus far in England teachers have not been subjected much to the tyranny of serving under an administrator who utilizes all the tools of business efficiency to keep them in line. The English school administrator typically doesn't know much about the theory of administration, and therefore the freedom of the teachers is increased. The headmaster is still boss, but without producing some of the harmful side effects that come from thinking of children and teachers as units in a conveyor-belt system of production.

One American historian of education has suggested that the lack of training in administration has been a factor in making headmasters and head teachers significant agents of educational innovation in contrast to their American counterpart, the school principal.

> For the circumscribed role that American principals have accepted and assumed has left them more often functionaries than teachers, more bureaucrats than professionals. It is hard to imagine them, or their colleagues in the educational establishment, leading a pedagogical revolution of the sort that has happened in British primary schools.[32]

Yet, there was such a pedagogical revolution (the Progressive Education Movement) in the United States stretching over several decades of the twentieth century and parts of that revolution were led by members of the educational establishment, including some principals and school superintendents.[33] Moreover, in England most head teachers or headmasters are not in "open" or progressive schools. In fact, there are many "old fashion" heads who resist innovation and change.[34] Where there are innovative practices the head teachers must share credit with classroom teachers who ventured out on their own in some cases and Her Majesty's Inspectors who spread the word of new methods and curricula.[35]

Some observers cite the general uniformity of curriculum in American schools as evidence that principals are exerting very little leadership in the area of curriculum innovation. English schools seem to differ more, even within the same county, or so it appears to American observers.[36]

Each school in England is still encouraged to develop a sense of uniqueness with which pupils (and teachers) can identify. Yet, at the end of the 1960s pupils in state-supported secondary schools began to emulate students in higher education by protesting. Thus was born a new challenge to the headmaster's authority as pupils began to demand a share in the decision-making process in their school.

Pupil Power

Some of the protesting pupils formed a national organization called the Schools Action Committee. Beginning in 1969 the *Times Educational Supplement* was filled with articles and letters to the editor for and against "pupil power." (The English use the term "pupil" for those in secondary schools and "student" for those in higher education.) Those in favor talked about the need for councils for each school, with large pupil representation. Those opposed spoke of "cracking down," getting rid of troublemakers, and so on.

Letters to the editor generally indicated opposition to pupil power. The letters varied in the degree of harshness with which pupil power was denounced. The following two letters are fairly typical of those critical of the movement.[37]

> Sir,—Your front page comment on the attempted suppression of the Schools Action Committee suggests that any such attempt is foolish.

I think it is time that sanity took a hand in these time-wasting antics and would hope that school authorities deal firmly with silly demands for pupil power.

The concept of pupil power, implying some sort of democratic rule in schools, is not one which will produce anything more profitable than its slightly less ludicrous parent, that much discredited concept of student power.

If we do not wish to encourage in our schools the sort of mindless sloganizing and nihilistic aggression which is currently disfiguring our universities then the Schools Action Committee and anything like it should be remorselessly opposed.

* * *

Sir,—It is deplorable that your paper should express support for vandalism in education. In your Comment of April 25 you accuse certain headmasters of being "stupid" not only because they have attempted to suppress the pupil power movement in their schools, but also for being unsympathetic to its aims.

My impression is that pupil power, even if non-violent, is nevertheless aiming to disrupt the life and works of schools unless all decisions are democratically made. That being so, I would have thought that firm opposition to this movement is anything but stupid. If its proposals were implemented (and presumably this is what its supporters want) then the organization and teaching in schools would be arranged to conform entirely to the wishes of the pupils who would enjoy a numerical majority over the staff. This could lead to casual attendance at classes, demands for entertainment in lessons, a lack of cooperation in completing set work while the atmosphere of the coffee bar would permeate the life of a school. It would be extremely difficult for a teacher to insist on good standards of work or to extend the experience of the pupils in a way which might not be immediately attractive to them. The progress of the pupil power programme can only increasingly neutralize the educational impact of a school.

... When such a movement directly threatens the whole purpose of a school then those in charge surely have a duty to suppress it with firmness.

In 1971 the National Union of Teachers acknowledged the issue of pupil power but said that at this stage it preferred to concentrate its efforts toward the goal of gaining greater teacher participation in policy making.[38] The Inner London Teachers Association, on the other hand, took a stand in favor of young people being more aware of what was going on in schools, but opposed any wild or extreme demands by pupils. This stand was taken in June 1972 after London pupils went on strike in May to publicize their demand for greater pupil participation in the running of their schools.[39]

In 1972 several LEAs added pupils (and parents) to the board of governors for each secondary school, though typically the pupils were not given the right to vote. During that spring the Secretary of the Department of Education and Science expressed the view that it was illegal for pupils under eighteen to vote on these boards.[40]

The English hope to satisfy the demands for pupil power in a way which will not undermine the authority of the headmaster or of the board of governors, which is a rather unique device to maintain the separate integrity of each school.

Board of Governors

If the headmaster in England has a boss it is the board of governors of his school more than the chief education officer. Each school in England which receives government aid, whether public or church-related, must have a board of governors. (The term "board of governors" is intended here to include the boards of management in the elementary schools.)

On the surface the board of governors may seem to resemble what community control advocates in the United States favor—namely, that for each neighborhood there would be a group of interested lay people to make important decisions for the school as a reflection of the wishes and needs of the nearby community. In practice it has not worked out that way at all in England. The boards of governors, or managers, are required by law. People are appointed to these boards in a perfunctory manner, and the boards tend to exercise very little real power. No one pretends that they adequately represent the nearby community. In fact, these boards may be an example of how a good idea can be institutionalized and thus killed off!

The rules governing the operation of these boards are established by the LEA but must be approved by the Department of Education and Science. In some cases the LEA has assigned several schools to a single board of governors, but some in the profession frown on this as having the effect of limiting the autonomy of each school.[41]

Usually the boards have limited powers; for example, they have no right to dismiss any teacher, except the teacher of religion in "aided" church schools. Things are more often reported to the board of governors than referred for a decision, although with some boards the headmaster is expected to clear his budget requests with the board before submitting it to the county government.[42]

The relationship of the headmaster with his board varies with his forcefulness. A strong headmaster frequently finds the board of governors to be a valuable link with the community; in other cases friction may develop as a board becomes assertive.

The board of governors serves chiefly as an advisory body. It is not supposed to interfere with day-to-day organization of the school, with curriculum, or with teaching methods—by tradition these are the province of the headmaster. Similarly, textbooks are chosen by the headmaster, who may involve his teachers in the process if he so desires. Neither the local governments nor the national government select textbooks or prepare lists of approved books, as is the case in France.

There has been some criticism of the composition of these governing boards. From one quarter comes the comment that the "Establishment" is over-represented on these boards; i.e., that there are too many clergymen (of the Church of England), upper-middle-class "prominent" citizens, and so on. From a different quarter comes the complaint that the Education Committee of the LEA is over-represented on the boards of individual schools. Some fear of government interference lies behind such a criticism, plus the feeling that the boards should include more persons genuinely interested in that particular school.

The teachers' organizations in the 1960s began to demand that teachers be represented on the boards of governors. Opposition to the idea was voiced by the influential Plowden Report *(Children and Their Primary Schools)*, which grew out of a nationwide study of elementary schools by an ad hoc committee of well-known lay persons and educators under the chairmanship of Lady Plowden. The Plowden Report feared an undermining of the head teacher's authority if teachers were on the board of managers and in a position to challenge the head teacher.

> A head could be placed in an intolerable situation if one of his assistant teachers [England's term for a regular classroom teacher] was on the managing body of the school.[43]

The Plowden Report did recommend that teachers have access to the board of managers, and to the LEA officials—the implication was clearly that in many cases teachers don't have such access.

Parents, too, don't usually have access to the board of managers of elementary schools. In fact, the Plowden Report said that in most cases the names of members of the boards of managers are completely unknown to the parents. Moreover, parents don't know what the functions of the board of managers are, or how to approach the board.

Although the appointment of managers is a matter of public knowledge in as much as they must be confirmed by the education committee, few parents can have any idea as to their functions or of their right of access to them.[44]

Local parents often don't serve on the board of managers of an elementary school. Older persons of "status" are more likely to be appointed, along with members of the county council or of the LEA.

The Plowden Committee found that the "great majority" of LEAs favored the idea of parent representation on boards of managers when asked about it, and thought that their existing procedures allowed for the appointment of parents. Very few LEAs, however, had rules requiring the appointment of some parents to the boards. The Plowden Report urged that parents be appointed to the boards of managers of elementary schools.[45]

Early in the twentieth century the national Ministry of Education (called Board of Education at that time) reportedly encouraged the idea that each school have a board of governors in order to protect the headmasters from the local governmental authorities which were beginning to exercise bureaucratic control over schools.[46]

Under the act of 1944 each school receiving public tax money is to have a board of governors. In the case of the county schools, the LEA appoints all members of the board. For those church schools receiving the maximum amount of public tax money and public control ("controlled schools"), one-third of the board members are appointed by the church and two-thirds by the LEA. The "aided" church schools, which receive less tax money, are allowed to appoint two-thirds of the board of governors and the LEA the other third.

The board of governors for a secondary school typically will have more power than the board of managers for an elementary school. But in both cases the boards often have less power than people suppose.[47]

The powers of the governors include the drawing up of an

annual financial estimate (budget) for their school. Reportedly this is often "almost meaningless" since the county allocates money automatically to each school on a formula basis.[48] Moreover, in most elementary schools the board of managers is not allowed to draw up the annual estimate of expenditures.

The chief duty of the board of governors is to be represented on the committee which appoints the teachers for that school; the headmaster sits on that committee and is usually influential, and a representative of the chief education officer also serves on the committee. The final word on any staff appointment lies with the LEA.

The board of governors may have a measure of control over curriculum in that they reflect public opinion and on occasion oppose certain innovations, while at other times they may press for the introduction of certain topics into the curriculum.

In cases of serious disputes, the influence of the board of governors in giving or withholding support for a headmaster can be sizable, especially in the case of a village school as compared to a city school.[49]

Teachers indicate some doubt as to the wisdom of boards of governors becoming active in school matters.[50] In the case of elementary school teachers the Plowden Report found that less than half of them thought the boards of managers were helpful.[51] NUT, in particular, has come out in opposition to boards of governors controlling curriculum, the appointment of teachers, or the granting of leaves of absence. Such matters, NUT asserts, should be left to the head teacher or to an academic board which should consist of members of the teaching staff. In addition, NUT would like to have teachers, parents, and the headmaster appointed to the board of governors.[52]

A similar suggestion has come from Simon Jenkins, a journalist. He advocates that boards of governors become advisory committees with no powers at all over the head teacher, though the head would be required to consult with the board and inform it of changes. The advantages of this new type of board, according to Jenkins, would be the elimination of politicians and the addition of interested community people who would cause the board to function in a vigorous way, in contrast to the present governors whose powers are eroding and who tend to abandon their sense of responsibility.[53]

Even when the board of governors does assert itself it may be overruled by the LEA. This was the case in 1971 with the Shirley Secondary Modern School at Croydon where a thirteen-year-old boy was suspended by the headmaster for writing an "obscene" essay. The board of governors upheld the headmaster's actions but was overruled by the LEA, which reinstated the boy. The LEA argued that technically the board of governors was a unit of the LEA's Education Committee and subject to its control.[54]

In a 1972 case, a teacher in a Church of England secondary school (Sir John Cass Foundation and Church of England Secondary School) was fired for publishing some avant garde poems of his students without securing prior permission from the board of governors. He appealed to the LEA's Staff Appeals Committee and was reinstated. In this instance the board of governors refused to accept the decision of the LEA and the national government was asked to decide the matter.[55] Such a step would be unthinkable in the United States because the federal government has no tradition of deciding such matters and because churches are free to run their own schools. In England the church schools get public funds and are subject to local and national government control. It is true, of course, in the United States that the interested parties in an educational dispute can take the matter to the local courts for a decision, and in some cases it may end up in the federal courts for settlement.

Many potential disputes in England are headed off by adroit action of the chief education officer of the LEA. The chief education officer, or a member of his staff, often serves as clerk at the meetings of the board of governors and acts as a go-between with the LEA.

Chief Education Officer

All LEAs are required to appoint a chief education officer. The list of candidates must be shown to the head of the national Department of Education and Science, who can strike names off the list. The chief education officer of the LEA is almost always a university graduate and has usually had teaching experience, though nowhere are specific requirements for the job laid down by law.

The office of chief education officer is roughly comparable to that of superintendent of schools in the larger cities of the United States. While the chief education officer has considerable power, he operates in a framework where some of the major problems which bother his American counterpart— such as determination of salaries—are settled at a higher level. Moreover, the chief education officer does not really have a group of teachers working for him; instead, the teachers regard themselves as working for, or with, the headmaster of their particular school.

The chief education officer in some of the LEAs has a staff of inspectors of schools (sometimes called advisers) who offer help to schools which seek it, and assist the chief education officer in evaluating the schools' budget requests.

It is unlikely that anyone in England would describe the role of the chief education officer in the way the job of superintendent of schools in the United States is described in a statement by the Educational Policies Commission of the National Education Association.

> The superintendency of schools is one of the most crucial and perhaps most difficult public positions in American life today.

The occupant of this position, more than any other single person in the community, influences the shape of public education.[56]

The Educational Policies Commission goes on to add that the superintendent of a local school system must be "politician, philosopher, student of life, public relations counsellor, and businessman." Moreover, he must be "a man who is at home in the world of ideas" and one who has "a thirst for learning throughout his professional career."[57] The chief education officer in England is viewed in less pretentious terms, perhaps because he is not expected to formulate a philosophy of education to undergird his school system. In fact, he is not seen as having a school system.

Historically, the chief education officer was seen as the adversary of the national school inspectors (the HMIs) and as the LEA's watchdog to guard against national government control. At the same time, as ex-teachers they tended to defend the teacher's autonomy (especially on curriculum matters) from interference by the local government.[58]

Yet in the 1950s and 1960s the chief education officer was an important part of a process of bureaucratization whereby teachers and headmasters were made to fit into a *system* of education. The growing emphasis on economic planning and national coordination created a flood of circulars, memos, reports, and the like. The chief education officer changed from a kind of glorified clerk to an administrator with the power to require reports from headmasters. In the process, what little power was left at the local level has been reallocated subtly at the expense of the headmasters and boards of governors.

> Traditionally, the English grammar school has been organized as a dictatorship, benevolent or otherwise. Once appointed, the headmaster has been supreme.... Today, the situation in the maintained grammar school is considerably different ... the head is responsible to the governors for the curriculum, the organization of the school and the welfare of the pupils. In many areas,

however, governors have little power and provide a facade behind which the Education Committee or even the Director of Education [Chief Education Officer] exercise effective control.[59]

The chief education officer has the authority to step in if any head teacher fails to follow the directives laid down by the LEA, but head teachers tend to see themselves as "autonomous" in regard to the chief education officer. This viewpoint has been interpreted as a sign of the lack of heavy-handed authoritarianism in the administration of English schools. The relationship of head teacher to chief education officer typically is free and easy. Moreover, it is rare for a head teacher to be dismissed by the LEA, but it can, and does on occasion, bring pressure to bear to force him to change.[60]

Headmasters and head teachers have a fair amount of discretionary power, but the fact that practices in schools within an LEA often are rather similar suggests that someone at the center of the county, or county borough, is exercising a standardizing influence—acting as "a common source of policy and inspiration."[61]

In some LEAs the chief education officer decides the order of priority of new school buildings being proposed to the national government; in other LEAs the Education Committee makes this decision, though usually on the basis of recommendations from the chief education officer. Some LEAs also allow the chief education officer to bargain with the Department of Education and Science to try to get additional allocations for their building programs.[62]

Chief education officers do seek to improve the educational program of the counties and cities where they are located, and a few have been identified with well-known educational innovations, such as Stewart Mason of Leicestershire and Alec Clegg of The West Riding. Sometimes, however, the chief education officer may not have a voice in deciding important matters of policy.[63] At other times, as in the case of Gateshead in the period from 1964 to 1967 when it was moving to a system of comprehensive schools, the chief education officer plays an active role in policy making.[64]

Yet the chief education officer lacks many of the powers which a strong educational leader would need. Attention was drawn to this lack of power at the end of the 1960s as a few areas (for example West Riding) gave their chief education officer the new freedom of spending up to £500 ($1200) per year without securing the prior approval of the Education Committee of the LEA.[65]

Recent parental pressure for a greater say about educational matters has also highlighted the relative lack of power of the chief education officer. When faced with angry citizens the chief education officer tends to reply that he doesn't make policy. The American school superintendent caught in the midst of a racial integration controversy or community unrest over the introduction of sex education, or other controversial topics, may try to shift the blame to the school board, or even to the national government, but usually without much success. The chief education officer is seldom fired while superintendents of schools are frequently fired after a relatively short tenure of office.

In the 1970s the office of chief education officer faces a new threat in that LEAs are being urged to appoint an important outsider as Ombudsman to arbitrate disputes between citizens and the LEA. In 1972, the chief education officers, through their association (Society of Education Officers), spoke out against the ombudsman concept. It would lead, they said, to chief education officers trying to avoid making decisions for fear of being overruled or being made to look bad by appeals to the ombudsman. As a result everything would be dropped in the lap of the Education Committee of the LEA to decide, including many petty matters best handled by an administrative official, such as the chief education officer. The Society of Education Officers also pointed out that under the 1944 Act citizens had the right to appeal to the national government (Department of Education and Science) and that many such appeals are made and the national government then conducts a detailed investigation.[66]

The future status of the chief education officer may depend to a considerable extent on how the national government implements the Maud Report on reorganization of local governments. NUT sees in the Report a tendency to downgrade the post of chief education officer, and as a result has already taken a stand against that feature.[67]

The future development of the LEAs will have an important influence on the role played by the teachers' groups and the national government in the decision-making process for the educational enterprise.

NOTES

1. The term "headmaster" will be used here as interchangeable with "head teacher" even though the former term is used most often in academic secondary schools (grammar schools), and in private schools.
2. George Baron, "Some Aspects of the Headmasters Tradition," p. 90 in P. W. Musgrave, *Sociology, History and Education*. London: Methuen, 1970.
3. George Baron, "Background Issues in Educational Administration," p. 111 in Baron, et. al., eds., *Educational Administration: International Perspectives*. Chicago: Rand McNally, 1969.
4. Baron, "Some Aspects," op. cit., p. 190.
5. Frank Musgrove, *Patterns of Power and Authority in English Education*. London: Methuen, 1971, pp. 4-5.
6. Frances M. Stevens, *The Living Tradition: The Social and Educational Assumptions of the Grammar School*. London: Hutchinson, 1960, p. 46.
7. H. C. Dent, *The Educational System of England and Wales*. London: Univ. of London Press, 1961, p. 87.
8. Anthony Sampson, *Anatomy of Britain Today*. New York: Harper and Row, 1965, p. 205.
9. Robert J. Fisher, *Learning How to Learn: The English Primary*

School and American Education. New York: Harcourt, Brace and Jovanovich, 1972, pp. 55-56.
  10. Maurice Kogan, *The Government of Education.* New York: Citation, 1971, p. 32.
  11. Seymour B. Sarason, *The Culture of the School and the Problem of Change.* Boston: Allyn and Bacon, 1971, pp. 141-142.
  12. Musgrave, op. cit., p. 70.
  13. Harry Davies, *Culture and the Grammar School.* London: Routledge and Kegan Paul, 1965, p. 84.
  14. Fisher, op. cit., p. 57.
  15. Harry A. Passow, *Secondary Education for ALL: The English Approach.* Columbus: Ohio State Univ. Press, 1961, p. 223.
  16. Central Advisory Council for Education (England). *Children and their Primary Schools,* Vol. I. London: Her Majesty's Stationery Office, 1967, p. 417.
  17. Ibid., pp. 417-418.
  18. Ibid., p. 333.
  19. Kogan, op. cit., pp. 27-28.
  20. Sarason, op. cit., pp. 127-128.
  21. *Children and Their Primary Schools,* op. cit., p. 333.
  22. Times Educational Supplement (London), October 24, 1969, p. 3.
  23. Ibid., March 28, 1969, p. 1023.
  24. Ibid., April 10, 1970, p. 10.
  25. Ibid., January 15, 1971, p. 3.
  26. Edmund J. King, *Other Schools and Ours,* third ed. New York: Holt, Rinehart and Winston, 1967, p. 109.
  27. Derek Birley, *The Education Officer and His World.* London: Routledge and Kegan Paul, 1970, p. 41.
  28. Times Educational Supplement (London), May 14, 1971, p. 8.
  29. Ibid., April 10, 1970, p. 10.
  30. Paul E. Peterson, "The Politics of Educational Reform in England and the United States." Comparative Education Review, Vol. 17, No. 2, June 1973, p. 175. Peterson cites Michael Steinman, "English Primary School Headteachers: The Role of a Professional Subgroup in a Formal Organization." Ph.D. dissertation, Univ. of Chicago, 1971, p. 218. See also Times Educational Supplement (London), January 16, 1970, p. 7.
  31. Ian Weinberg, *The English Public Schools: The Sociology of Elite Education.* New York: Atherton, 1967, p. 78.
  32. Michael Katz in the introduction to Kogan, *The Government of Education,* op. cit., pp. 8-9.

33. See Lawrence A. Cremin, *The Transformation of the School.* New York: Random House, 1961.
34. Fisher, op. cit., p. 51.
35. Lilian Weber, *The English Infant School and Informal Education.* Englewood Cliffs, N.J.: Prentice-Hall, 1971, pp. 44-45, 147-149.
36. Fisher, op. cit., p. 52.
37. Times Educational Supplement (London), May 9, 1969, p. 1541.
38. National Union of Teachers of England and Wales. *Teacher Participation: A Study Outline.* London: NUT, 1971, p. 9.
39. Times Educational Supplement (London), June 16, 1972, p. 10.
40. Ibid., June 30, 1972, p. 7.
41. H. C. Dent, *The Education Act, 1944,* fifth ed. London: Univ. of London Press, 1955, p. 31; and Davies, op. cit., p. 84.
42. Kogan, op. cit., p. 35.
43. *Children and their Primary Schools,* op. cit., p. 416.
44. Ibid., p. 415.
45. Ibid.
46. Baron, "Some Aspects," op. cit., p. 190.
47. Birley, op. cit., p. 41.
48. Ibid.
49. Kogan, op. cit., p. 35.
50. Times Educational Supplement (London), June 27, 1969, p. 2119.
51. *Children and their Primary Schools,* op. cit., p. 414.
52. *Into the 70's,* op. cit., pp. 26-27.
53. Times Educational Supplement (London), June 27, 1969, p. 2107.
54. Ibid., May 14, 1971, p. 3.
55. Ibid., July 7, 1972, p. 6.
56. Educational Policies Commission, *The Unique Role of the Superintendent of Schools.* Washington, D.C.: National Education Assn., 1965, p. 1.
57. Ibid., p. 7, 23.
58. History of Education Society (England), *Studies in the Government and Control of Education Since 1860.* London: Methuen, 1970, p. 7.
59. Davies, op. cit., p. 83.
60. Kogan, op. cit., pp. 25-30.
61. Ibid., p. 29.
62. John A. Griffith, *Central Departments and Local Authorities.* Toronto, Can.: Univ. of Toronto Press, 1966, p. 134.

63. Ibid., pp. 118, 127-128, 134.

64. Richard Bately, Oswald O'Brien, and Henry Parris, *Going Comprehensive: Educational Policy-Making in Two County Boroughs.* London: Routledge and Kegan Paul, 1970, pp. 96-97.

65. Times Educational Supplement (London), March 7, 1969, p. 701.

66. Ibid., July 21, 1972, p. 3.

67. *Into the 70's,* op. cit., p. 24.

Chapter 6

THE DEATH OF LOCAL INITIATIVE

Local government is a cherished institution in England, but by the late 1960s there was much talk of the lack of vitality at the local level. Nowhere was this more evident than in the field of education where encroachments by the national government threatened the few remaining prerogatives of the counties and cities.

In England the counties and the large cities have been the basic units in the administration of schools. Each county is designated a Local Education Authority (LEA), as are the larger cities. For all of England, which covers 50,056 square miles and includes approximately 46 million people, there are 145 LEAs. In addition, several of the LEAs have districts with partial autonomy; there are 125 of these "divisional executives." Then there are 31 "excepted districts" exercising partial control over their schools in accordance with the Education Act of 1944. All together there are about 300 units of local government dealing with education; this compares with some 15,000 school districts in the United States, which has a population four times that of England. The LEAs have banded together to form the Association of Education Committees, which actively represents the interests of the LEAs to the national government and typically opposes attempts of the national government to extend central control over education.[1]

Educators in England differ in their estimations of the viable power of local governments in regard to schools. Maurice Kogan, a university professor of social sciences, describes the powers of the national government mainly as constraints imposed on local governments in certain specified areas, such as school building finance. He suggests that the fate of innovation and reform depends to a considerable degree on the attitude of the LEAs.

> The real say over schools, the power to make or break an educational pattern, however, rests with the LEAs.[2]

However, Edmund King, university professor of education, notes the difficulties of new ideas and innovations in education taking root and asserts that "innovation and modernization are far beyond the scope—or comprehension—of many local bodies [LEAs]."[3] In a major study of the relationship of local governments to the national government, John A. G. Griffith argues that while the national government influences local governments, the reverse is also true. He asserts that many of the important advances made by the national government originate with local governments.[4]

The differences between LEAs in the provision of education suggest that the LEA does make a difference. Certainly educational policy differs depending on which political party controls the LEA. Thus, comprehensive schools tend to thrive in LEAs controlled by the Labor Party.[5]

At the end of the 1950s a leading English economist, Sir Geoffrey Crowther, visited the United States and observed publicly that in the United States there was more local control over education than was the case in England.⁶ Events of the last few years have widened the gap, mainly because of the sizable growth of national government intervention in England.

In part, the differences between the two countries relate to the fact that public schools in the United States are run usually by persons whose children go to these schools. When they legislate on education they are dealing with their own children not the children of a different—and lower—social group. The notable exception to the rule are those school districts where the schools have become largely Black in population and the school board remains largely, or entirely, white. It should also be noted that American sociologists have long criticized the overrepresentation of middle-class persons on school boards, even though most of them are elected to office. In England many members of boards dealing with education are themselves a product of private schools and often send their children to private schools.

Local governments in England levy taxes for local services (including schools) without consulting the voters via a referendum, as is frequently the case in the United States; so the LEA is relatively free of citizen pressure. The LEA, however, is closely controlled by one or the other of the two major political parties so that educational policy reflects the views of the dominant political party.⁷

Members of the county and city councils in England are elected to that office (usually representing one of the major political parties) and for the purposes of administering education function as LEAs. Since these county and city councils also administer roads and other public services, they delegate educational matters to the Education Committee, composed mainly of members of the LEA, plus usually a number of prominent local citizens selected by the LEA. All LEAs are expected to consult their Education Committees prior to making policy decisions. The LEA may delegate various powers to the Education Committee, except the right to borrow money or to raise the tax rate.⁸ Within budgetary limits, Education Committees are given a certain amount of freedom to operate.

The Education Committees vary in size, from those with only 5 members to some with 50 or more members; 20 to 30 members is fairly common, which is larger than a typical school board in the United States.

Each of the LEAs operates its own elementary, secondary and vocational schools, in addition to teacher-training colleges ("colleges of education") and technical colleges at the higher education level. Some of the LEAs (less than half) have a corps of inspectors, who offer inservice courses for teachers and handle minor administrative matters.

The LEA has the power to veto proposed new facilities for the church schools, but the national government has the final say. The LEA appoints the teachers for the county schools, but the number of teachers to be employed and the salaries they will receive are determined at the national level, as are a good many matters of educational policy. Under this system the individual school is insulated somewhat from public pressure, as are the teachers.

The present system dates back to the Education Act of 1902 which ended England's 32-year (1870-1902) experiment with small school districts. There were several hundred of these districts, each with its publicly-elected school board. This school board era generated fierce political partisanship and often pitted one religious group against another, since the church schools (mainly Church of England and Catholic) were meeting vigorous competition from public schools, supported by most of the other church groups and by the secularists. All of this grass-roots activity proved too unsettling to the upper classes, who were willing to provide a measure of schooling for the masses but were unused to the idea of ordinary people having a say about educational matters.

A parallel development occurred in the United States around 1900 as progressives and persons interested in

The Death of Local Initiative

efficiency sought to end some of the "excessive decentralization" found in the big cities where school board members were elected to represent wards, or neighborhoods, in the city. Often these wards were dominated by certain ethnic groups. To get the schools out of ethnic politics, central school boards were created in several big cities, with the members elected-at-large to represent the whole city. At the same time much power was turned over to the superintendent of schools, a newly emerging professional.[9]

The Education Act of 1902 in England ended the local school districts and took the county as the basic unit (LEA) for administering education. In those LEAs with subunits ("divisional executives") the smaller units have some control over school attendance, school upkeep, and the like. The chief education officer of these subunits is responsible to the chief education officer of the LEA.

The LEAs only provide 40 percent of the funds for schools; the other 60 percent comes from the national government. Funds granted by the national government go first to the local governments in the form of a block grant, and the local governments have the power to decide how much of this block grant will go for schools, for roads, and so forth. The 40 percent contributed for education by the local governments is raised by local real estate taxes, or "rates" as they are called.

One of the major tasks of the LEAs is to determine the educational needs of their areas and to propose the construction of a specific number of schools to meet that need. The Department of Education and Science examines the building program submitted by the LEAs and approves or rejects them; it also specifies cost limitations and issues regulations for the use of its funds in school construction or alterations. Within the limits set by the national government guidelines, the LEAs are free to specify the design of the school buildings, and English educators are proud of the number of well-designed buildings which have resulted.[10]

The grant from the national government to an LEA for general operating expenses takes into account not only the number of pupils in the county, but also the local tax rate and the educational need of the area. In this way the national grants seek to equalize some of the inequalities in educational opportunity which exist between different parts of England.

The LEAs vary greatly in size, in population, and in financial means. London covers 117 square miles as compared to Lancashire's 2,000 square miles. Birmingham has a population of over 1 million, while the LEA of Rutland has under 30,000 people. Some of the wealthy LEAs have 100 times the financial resources of other LEAs.[11]

The national government's grant goes to the county council, and the council, rather than the Education Committee, decides how much will go for education. Some county councils delegate a set amount to the Education Committee and allow it to decide how the money will be spent. In other LEAs every expenditure approved by the Education Committee must be approved by the full city or county council, or by its finance committee. The Education Committee lost some of the power in 1958 when the national government changed over to the block grant system, with national funds no longer earmarked for education.[12]

There is some evidence that Education Committees in LEAs often fool with petty items best left to the chief education officer.[13] On the other hand, the Education Committee often has to struggle to preserve a measure of independence from the county council, and from the political parties which lurk behind the elected councilmen. In this bid for autonomy the Education Committee has the support of the National Union of Teachers (NUT).

The LEA, in turn, has been struggling to maintain its viability in the face of growing pressure from a variety of sources to curtail some of its functions. One of the most serious threats was the proposal from the Robbins Report (1963) that the teachers' colleges be taken from the LEAs, perhaps to come under more direct supervision of the universities. The LEAs individually spoke out against the proposal, as did their Association of Education Committees. (This Association has been described as the counterpart of the American School Board Association but reportedly carries more weight than the American organization.)[14] The national government chose not to implement this part of the Robbins Report—not so much out of respect for local autonomy but more because university-sponsored education was expensive and England at the time was in the midst of financial troubles.[15] The local governments did lose one of their higher education institutions, however, when the national government upgraded the colleges of advanced technology to university status and granted them autonomy.

At the end of the 1960s the heads of the technical and vocational schools issued a statement calling for the removal of such institutions from LEA control and placement of them under regional authorities to be created for that purpose; each regional authority would include several counties.[16]

At about the same time a national commission (Maud Commission) was appointed to study the question of reorganization of local governments. In 1969 the Maud Commission indicated grave concern about the future of local government.

> ... the prospect for local government is bleak. Local governors... cannot grapple effectively with their problems.... During the next decade, unless the system is reformed local government will be increasingly discredited and will be gradually replaced by agencies of central government.[17]

Most of the groups testifying before the Maud Commission urged that the power of the national government over education be reduced and that the powers of local governments be increased.[18] The Maud Report endorsed the premise that unless the number of units of local government was reduced, and the new units made more efficient, local government would wither away and the drift toward national government control would continue.

The Maud Report suggested that the existing LEAs be reduced to 78 units (58 unitary districts combining rural and urban, and 20 metropolitan districts). The Report claimed that under this new arrangement there would be more freedom and power for the individual school's board of governors, or board of managers. Moreover, the Report added, "we are confident that ways of doing this can be found which avoid interference with the proper responsibilities of heads and other teachers."[19]

NUT's response to the Maud Report was to note that the proposed units of local government would be bigger and stronger than before and that in negotiating with them the teachers' organizations would have to present a united front.[20] The idea of getting all the teachers' organizations into one camp was an old idea with NUT, but was viewed with caution by the smaller teachers' groups, notably the National Association of Schoolmasters.

In an editorial, the *Times Educational Supplement* saw the Maud Report as downgrading the Education Committees in LEAs since the stress would be on treating education, roads, and other county services all together. In fact, there would no longer be a legal requirement that counties have an Education Committee. The result would be that more power over education would accumulate in the hands of bureaucrats in local government, and these were not necessarily people interested in education. As the *Times Educational Supplement* saw it, there must be a strong representative of education in the local governments to negotiate with the strong teachers' groups, or there will be trouble.[21]

It was clear by 1972 that the legal obligation of each LEA to appoint an Education Committee was to be preserved, but the powers to be delegated to such Education Committees were still under study. The likelihood of the Education

Committees getting more autonomy than at present is reduced by the prevailing spirit of the reorganization plan which is to have the LEAs run in a centralized, more tightly controlled way.[22]

Also by 1972 the national government was talking about 93 units for England; namely, 38 counties (having a total of 27 million people), 34 metropolitan districts (12 million people), 20 suburban districts around London (5 million people) and the inner city of London (3 million). Only 23 of the units would have a population under 250,000.[23]

The Maud Report is to be implemented in the mid-1970s. Meanwhile, considerable diversity remains among the LEAs. Some LEAs still use the eleven-plus examination to select applicants for secondary education and some do not; some have a complete system of comprehensive schools and some do not; some of the LEAs have schools filled mainly with middle-class children and some tend to have mostly working-class children.

The plans made for raising the compulsory school age to sixteen in the fall of 1972 illustrate the diversity still existing among the LEAs. The national government issued a circular in August 1971 asking each LEA to submit a plan for handling the fifteen-year-olds who would now remain in school. There was considerable variety in the plans submitted. Some of the LEAs planned new buildings, others were going to have new kinds of classrooms, such as "seminar-tutorial," project rooms, study rooms, library areas, and so on. Some of the LEAs tied in their plans with the National Youth Service agency, and others with existing vocational schools. Some measure of uniformity came from the fact that many of the curriculum changes reflected research done by the Schools Council. Yet, the range of courses was wide—all the way from cosmetology to new social studies, and from human relations to courses involving outdoor camps and mountain climbing.[24]

Not everyone views diversity as desirable, especially if it

means that in some schools there is inadequate educational opportunity. The Labor Party took such a stand in July 1972 in a policy statement.

> If the pupils of a particular school consistently fall far short of the normal achievements for their age-group, the local authority must be required to make proposals for remedying the deficiency.[25]

It is the national government, of course, which the Labor Party has in mind to bring the particular LEA into line.

More diversity and a step toward returning a bit of power to the LEAs is implicit in the decision of the Department of Education and Science in 1972 to add another 19 LEAs to the original five who were allowed, on a trial basis, to decide their own priorities for school buildings without having to justify each project to the national government. A spirit of caution prevails, however, and when the LEA for the heart of London announced in the fall of 1972 its plans to expand its nursery school facilities to accommodate 6500 more children, it added that the project was dependent on securing national government approval.[26]

Fear persists that local governments are doomed unless new, and probably larger, units are created. Meanwhile control over education continues to slip away from the LEAs. The latest threat comes from an outpouring of citizen protest about schools and citizen pressure for change. This upsurge of lay interest in educational policy is relatively new in England and poses a challenge to the professionals and to the government bureaucrats alike.

NOTES

1. John A. Griffith, *Central Departments and Local Authorities.* Toronto, Can.: Univ. of Toronto Press, 1966, p. 43.
2. Maurice Kogan, *The Government of Education.* New York: Citation, 1971, p. 22.

3. Edmund J. King, *Other Schools and Ours*, 4th ed. New York: Holt, Rinehart and Winston, 1973, p. 194.
4. Griffith, op. cit., p. 18.
5. See the case of Darlington, England described in Richard Batley, Oswald O'Brien, and Henry Parris, *Going Comprehensive; Educational Policy-Making in Two County Boroughs*. London: Routledge and Kegan Paul, 1970, pp. 23-60.
6. Sir Geoffrey Crowther, "Contrasts in British and American Education," in *Major Speeches Delivered at the Conference of Maryland High School Principals and Supervisors*, Oct. 8 and 9, 1959, Baltimore: Maryland Dept. of Education, 1959, p. 32.
7. Batley, et. al., op. cit., pp. 23-33, 74; and Paul E. Peterson, "The Politics of Educational Reform in England and the United States." Comparative Education Review, Vol. 17, No. 2, June 1973, pp. 176-177.
8. Theodore L. Reller and E. L. Morphet, *Comparative Educational Administration*. Englewood Cliffs, N.J.: Prentice-Hall, 1962, p. 61.
9. Frederick M. Wirt and Michael W. Kirst, *The Political Web of American Schools*. Boston: Little, Brown, 1972, pp. 5-9.
10. Kogan, op. cit., p. 16.
11. H. C. Dent. *The Educational System of England and Wales*. London: Univ. of London Press, 1961, p. 78. In the 1960s the London LEA was broken up into several LEAs.
12. Derek Birley, *The Education Officer and His World*. London: Routledge and Kegan Paul, 1970, p. 27.
13. Ibid., pp. 37-38.
14. James D. Koerner, *Reform in Education: England and the United States*. New York: Delacorte, 1968, p. 31.
15. William Taylor, *Society and the Education of Teachers*. London: Faber and Faber, 1969, p. 77.
16. Times Educational Supplement. (London), May 16, 1969, p. 1624.
17. Ibid., June 13, 1969, p. 1955.
18. Ibid., June 6, 1969, p. 1873.
19. Ibid., June 13, 1969, p. 1943.
20. Ibid., June 13, 1969, p. 1946.
21. Ibid., June 20, 1069, p. 2045.
22. Ibid., July 14, 1972, p. 2.
23. Ibid., July 21, 1972, p. 2.
24. Department of Education and Science, *Reports on Education*, March 1972, No. 73, pp. 1-4.
25. Times Educational Supplement (London), July 14, 1972, p. 2.
26. Ibid.

Chapter 7

GRASSROOTS DEMOCRACY

Schools are responsible to the people, according to the American ideology, and a system of public schools has been developed to implement the concept. The advantages of the system seem self-evident to people in the United States reared on the doctrine of political democracy—American style. The disadvantages of the system are recognized in extreme cases, as, for example, when the Los Angeles school board after World War II, speaking in the name of the people, tried to stop the public schools from teaching about the United Nations and its affiliate, the United Nations Educational, Scientific and Cultural Organization (UNESCO).

Some of the disadvantages of the American system are subtle and involve the ways in which professionals (teachers) respond to public pressure by asserting authoritarian control over the children.

The fact that teachers must answer directly to the public for their activities means that they will retain firm control over the process of inquiry and expression in the classroom to insure that *they themselves* will not be punished by an irate public—which according to the folklore, is sovereign in matters of education. Although the methods of punishment may differ, for example, vetoing the school bond issue, a negative performance report, and so on, the teacher is vulnerable to the judgment of the public in the same way that the student is vulnerable to the judgment of the teacher. For the public holds the teacher's reputation in escrow until it is satisfied that he will control the student's intellectual and character development in a way acceptable to the dominant group in the community.[1]

The argument for teacher independence hinges on the claim that the teacher is a professional and to do his job effectively must be left alone. Efficiency in education does depend on professionalism, and lay control amounts to interference with the professional. Yet, advocates of more community control over schools see a connection between education being relevant and the assertiveness of lay citizens.

Teachers at one point may have dreamed of complete professional independence, but the time is past when any one segment of society can control an institution as important as the school. Eric Hoffer, among others, has stressed this point.

There is a change of climate now taking place everywhere which is unfavorable to the exercise of absolute power. Even in totalitarian countries the demand of common folk are becoming determining factors in economic, social, and political decisions.[2]

The demand by citizens in both England and the United States for more involvement with their schools is related to the growing loss of community feeling as people leave the small communities to be swallowed up in urban areas, or in the shapeless and rootless suburbia. In England this is mitigated somewhat by the intimacy that follows from the smallness of the country and of the schools, compared to the United States.

Involvement with local institutions is a way of establishing roots and achieving a sense of identity. In England such participation runs headlong into a long-standing tradition that parents should not interfere with the headmaster or his teachers.

In recent times the tradition of parental non-interference and general aloofness from the day-to-day operation of the school had changed considerably, particularly as compared to the nineteenth century. Even in the early years of the twentieth century in England the gates to school yards, once the children were inside, were locked to keep the parents out.[3] Today, parents are more welcome at the schools, particularly on "open days" when parents are encouraged to visit.

Parent-teacher associations exist in some schools, though occasionally a headmaster will ban such an organization on the ground that it might interfere with school matters. Some headmasters fear that parent-teacher associations will be dominated by a particular political party and endanger the goodwill established between the school and governmental authorities.

School administrators in England until recently have felt relatively secure in a system buttressed by tradition and one where their prerogatives are respected. Those school administrators who visited schools in the United States in the 1950s were appalled at what they called excessive demands put on the American school administrator by parents and other citizens. This was a time when there was much criticism of American schools in terms of the low academic tone; at the same time critics lashed out at any attempt by teacher and pupils to analyze controversial issues.[4] During the same decade, teachers in England felt that they were relatively free in their choice of materials and methods, and they attributed this to the English pattern of educational administration.

> To a large extent the English pattern of education administration protects the schools from direct and conscious political and social

pressures. The link between the various levels of the educational structure are so strong and numerous that any attempt by local or national interest to influence the teaching in the schools has to contend with established opinion within the universities, the Ministry [of Education], and the teachers' associations.... The schools, therefore, have been assured of freedom from inquisitorial investigations, a freedom which has helped to develop a keen sense of responsibility for an unbiased though not a colourless treatment of subject matter.[5]

An American professor's wife who spent one year in Oxford in the late 1950s was struck by the English school's freedom from citizen interference.

We could do with a little more of this hand-off attitude at home ... More respect for the educator's professional opinion. Fewer courses of study written into law by legislators under the influence of citizen pressure groups. Less assumption by individual citizens that the school exists to serve their individual child ... But on the other hand, the fact that we Americans think of the schools as ours to control makes them much more responsive to changing needs.[6]

There is far less talk in England about the right of people to control their institutions, such as schools. This may be because the belief in democracy is less strong than in the United States, or perhaps it is just defined differently. The following statement made in England in 1963 was not untypical for the time and is a baseline against which to measure the subsequent progress toward citizen control:

England in the 1960s is an aristocratic society, not a democratic one. That is the main fact to be realized if its system of education is to be fully understood. The majority of its citizens still believe in aristocracy (government by the best people) rather than in democracy (government by all the people).[7]

The parental and citizen protest activities which developed in the 1960s seldom involved the content of education. There was, however, discontent with such matters as the way education was organized, and the question of whose children benefited most from the system. At the end of the 1960s and in the early 70s there was criticism of the free and open approach used in some schools, and especially the failure to teach children to read effectively. In addition, the autonomy of the teacher was reevaluated from the point of view of parents having some control over their children's education.

Two English scholars suggest that "during the past hundred years there has grown up in our midst a new despotism: the rule of teachers."[8] Up to the 1860s what was taught was determined by what the school's founder had specified, what the laws said, and what parents wanted. New private schools catered to the religious or social class preferences of the parents. The growing loss of parental influence was evident by the end of the nineteenth century, and was accelerated by the Education Act of 1902, which created LEAs remote from the parents and designed to act as a buffer between the school and the parents. The abolition of fee paying at the end of the 1930s ended one of the last vestiges of parent power.[9] (Usually the histories of English education describe the abolition of school fees as a step in the democratization of the educational system, on the ground that good education was no longer reserved to the wealthy.)

At the beginning of the 1960s the schools and teachers in England were relatively free of citizen pressure and were not preoccupied with strategies to please the parents. A few of the LEAs did take the time to print up brochures explaining the schools to parents whose children were entering elementary or secondary schools for the first time, and some of the LEAs held an annual "education week" with a program of speeches on education by local or national figures.[10]

After 1960, citizen interest in education quickened in England. Local groups of parents began to form Associations for the Advancement of State Education, at first to protest the lack of improvements in public elementary education and later to work for improvements at all levels of education. By

October 1962, there were 35 such local units spread throughout the country. From the beginning it was basically a middle class movement.

In 1963 these associations joined to form a national association and immediately embarked on a year-long campaign to publicize the needs of education. Week after week prominent individuals appeared at local meetings to speak about such matters as overcrowded classes, the shortage of teachers, and so on. The culmination was an "Education Week" in November 1963, which received wide publicity.

The wide support given to the 1963 campaign led to the formation of a permanent organization in 1964. This Confederation for the Advancement of State Education (CASE) seeks to be nonpolitical and yet to put pressure on political parties and the national government to produce educational improvements. The secretary of the organization declared in 1964 that "we will be out to arouse a national passion about education."[11]

It is difficult to judge the effectiveness of citizen associations in shaping educational policy, but it may be significant that the national government's Social Survey of 1965 added a series of questions to determine attitudes of parents toward various educational problems. Two years later educational issues were clearly a factor in national elections.[12]

While parents and interested citizens were beginning to act as a pressure group to influence educational policy, their effectiveness was circumscribed by certain ingredients in the English situation. In the first place, many things were decided at the national level; thus, parents had little or no control over the salaries paid teachers, the ratio of pupils to teachers, and the priorities for building new schools. In the second place, LEA officials and members of the boards of governors for individual schools did not encourage any activity which might appear to be a usurpation of their legal role in educational matters. In addition, there was the longstanding tradition of headmasters not encouraging parental activity. This tradition began to change in certain nursery and elementary schools which embarked on progressive or "open" approaches to education; typically, more parental involvement was seen as part of a more open-ended approach to learning.

Citizen interest in education in England coincided with rising expenditures on education. Costs were increasing not only because of burgeoning enrollments but also as a result of new emphases on science and technology, fields which were costly in equipment and facilities.

In a similar way, rising educational costs in the United States, in the 1950s, produced an outbreak of criticism of schools by citizen groups—often taxpayers' associations dedicated to economy in government and lower property taxes. At the same time prominent citizens rallied to form citizen associations to remind Americans of the need for quality education and the important role which public schools play in the shaping of a democratic society.

Beginning in the 1960s an attempt to eliminate remaining injustices in the United States, especially racial prejudice, led to federal grants designed to arouse local citizens to take an interest in social institutions. In education this has led to demands from civil rights groups that Negro parents have control over their neighborhood schools, even to the point of interviewing teachers to see if their attitudes are "right" in order to teach their children. Several cities are experimenting with administrative schemes of breaking the city into subdistricts with assistant superintendents in charge but advised by citizen advisory councils.

There is the additional factor of a general challenging of authority in the United States; this has led college students to demand a role in the running of their colleges, and Catholic parents to insist that the control of parochial schools no longer be the exclusive prerogative of the clergy. Several Catholic dioceses have added school boards made up of lay Catholics who share the control of policy formation with the local clergy. All of this represents a rather widespread feeling that people should have a greater share in controlling the important institutions which shape their lives. We even have welfare or dole recipients organizing and demanding a say in how relief money will be given to them.

In England at first it was middle-class parents who began to criticize the schools and educational policy generally. One explanation of this active interest in public schools (county schools run by the LEA) was that by the 1960s it was clear to the middle class that because of lack of money it would not be possible to buy a place for their child in one of the better private schools. As the *Times Educational Supplement* put it:

> Are the middle classes beginning to realize that willy-nilly the state system is theirs and that their children will go through it? Is it this that is determining them [middle class parents] to do something about it [state education]?[13]

From 1964 onward a storm of protest came from parents and citizens over the comprehensive school question. Some persons were demanding the establishment of comprehensive schools and an end to the harsh selection system which determined a child's fate at age eleven plus. Other people tended to defend the prestigious secondary schools (grammar schools) which their children were lucky enough to attend. In Bristol and Liverpool citizens not accustomed to protest activities took to the streets to march in demonstrations against comprehensive schools, and thousands signed petitions. In Ealing, in 1966, parents secured 10,000 signatures on a petition but failed to halt the introduction of comprehensive schools. They then took the matter to court, but the judge ruled against them saying that parental wishes were only one of a number of factors which LEAs had to consider in making decisions about schools. In Gateshead, in the period from 1964 to 1967, the LEA did not tell the local citizens much of anything about a new system of schools being introduced on the ground that there was little to tell until national government approval was secured. After approval was obtained there was still no attempt to inform parents in any systematic way, though a minority on the county council expressed the wish that parents be more involved in the whole business.[14]

The need for more citizen participation gradually was acknowledged in England, however, and professional educators revived an old pedagogical doctrine, especially popular in the United States, that parental and citizen "involvement" in education was a good thing.

Citizen involvement was discussed in the Plowden Report. The Plowden Committee was interested in parents, but not in terms of sharing in policy formation for schools. The relevant section of the Report is titled "Participation By Parents" and starts with the premise that the quality of the home affects the quality of the work done in school, so educators should involve the parents in the work of the school. The thirteen pages of the section[15] spoke in a very traditional tone of ways of encouraging parents to visit schools, of having "open days" for visits, of finding time for teachers to consult with a parent about Johnny's schoolwork, and of parents collecting money to buy equipment for the classrooms. Almost nothing was said about parental participation in decisions on curriculum, methods, and so on. The stress was on helping parents to understand how the school functions. This reminds one of the thread-bare "home-school relations" topic in books on education over the last forty years in the United States.

The single reference in the "Participation By Parents" section of the Plowden Report to policy making was a negative one, namely that some of the teachers and head teachers testifying before the Plowden Committee spoke of the Parent-Teacher Association (PTA) as an American importation and indicated some fear that the PTA might interfere with the running of the school. In the Report, the Plowden Committee members did say that in their visits to schools in the United States they found no example of PTAs "running the school." On the other hand, the Report saw some danger if PTAs were dominated by a small clique of parents.

The Plowden Report did not see the PTA as the best way to involve parents, and the better PTAs were described as those where "good leadership is given by the head [head teacher]."[16] Reportedly "heads are adept at pacifying parents individually, although they seem less secure when faced with the prospect of a large gathering; this is one reason that many remain chary of parent organizations."[17] Less than one-quarter of the elementary schools in England have parent-teacher associations, and as of 1968 there were about 70,000 parents and teachers enrolled in these associations.[18] In the United States there were 43,000 local PTA units and over 9 million members.[19]

The Plowden Committee said that in the course of holding hearings and gathering data it had found little demand for more participation by parents. Half of the parents did say that they would like better information on how their children were doing in school.[20]

Along the lines of providing information to parents—and that is what the section of parent participation is all about—the Plowden Report suggested that the LEA publish a booklet explaining the school. The idea is an old one to American school administrators who, from 1930 onward, got caught up in the mania for "public relations." In the United States the public relations approach was just one more sign of the school administrators' tendency to identify with the world of business.[21]

Where the Plowden Report cited parental dissatisfaction it had to do mainly with difficulty in getting to see the teacher; 90 percent of the parents reported this difficulty, and 70 percent said that teachers didn't seem particularly pleased when parents visited school. The Report urged that the schools encourage parents to visit their children's classrooms and talk to the teachers.

Getting parents to visit schools may not be anything like parents sharing in policy-making, but in a country like England, where social class barriers exist between the middle-class teacher and the working-class parent, it is an achievement to get them to come. This is especially true at the secondary school level, in the case of the grammar school.

Working-class parents with children in grammar schools often do not understand the school; they fear it, fail to visit the teachers, or feel ill at ease on those occasions when they do visit. A study by two Englishmen documented the problems in the following words:

> The school usually offered an annual opportunity for parents to consult teachers, and of course it was always possible to make an appointment with the head. Yet it was clear indeed that these opportunities were only taken up by the more prosperous, and by some of those who had had grammar school experience themselves.[22]

Working-class parents also find it difficult to participate in parent-teacher associations. A study done for the Plowden Committee found that with elementary school parents, 25 percent of the professional parents had attended one or more PTA meetings, but only 5 percent of the working-class parents had done so.[23]

In some ways parents are the same the world over with respect to schools. For example, the schools in the United States certainly are open to parents, yet many parents do not visit them. Moreover, lower-class parents are less likely to visit with teachers and, like their counterparts in England, tend to feel awkward and out of place in the school building.

There is probably some difficulty on the part of the professional to adjust to the life style of poor or lower-class parents. This had been the case in the United States as parents from slum areas of the inner city were recruited as "teacher aides;" friction often developed between such aides and the college-trained teacher in a traditional classroom.

In England the question of teacher aides has been viewed not so much as a vehicle for parental participation but rather as a source of cheap labor to do part of the teacher's job. Not surprisingly, the National Union of Teachers has opposed teachers' aides as an attempt to put cheap and unprofessional workers in competition with the trained teacher. NUT is even opposed to using parents to "hear children read."

A year after the Plowden Report appeared, the national government issued a pamphlet entitled *Parent-Teacher Relations in Primary Schools,* which further elaborated the concept of involving parents via visits to school, parents raising money for classroom equipment, parents helping to supervise children on field trips, and so on. The booklet contained "examples of good practice in parent-teacher relations." Of the dozens of real examples given of good parent-teacher relations only one came close to parental involvement in policy-making; this was a case of a head teacher and the deputy head sitting down with two members of the parent-teacher association and discussing new possibilities in curriculum and school organization.[24]

In spite of the cautious and traditional tone of both the pamphlet and the Plowden Report, parents and citizens asserted themselves aggressively about school matters. One such case occurred in Loughton, Essex when the parents at St. Nicholas County School fought to overturn the LEA's decision to close this elementary school. The parents claimed that over a three-year period all the decisions in regard to the future of the school had been made without consulting the parents. The chief education officer indicated that the LEA's decision was final but that in retrospect "it might perhaps have been wiser if parents had been consulted at an earlier stage."[25]

In Enfield, the Ealing Parent Association sent a letter to the national government (Secretary of the Department of Education and Science) denouncing the inadequate facilities in its fairly new comprehensive school. In addition, the parents challenged the whole secondary school reorganization plan for their area which the LEA had submitted to the national government.[26]

The protests in Sheffield involved both working-class parents and middle-class parents. The working-class parents demonstrated in front of the city hall in protest over the plan to close down the Wybourn School, which had impressed the parents with innovations such as team teaching and which had become a social center for this working-class district. The local press and the Member of Parliament representing the area came to the support of the protesters. At the same time another group of parents were holding meetings, demonstrating outside the same city hall to impress the members of the city council, and issuing pamphlets denouncing the overcrowded classes and inadequate facilities in the elementary schools. These middle-class parents were well-organized and impressed the chief education officer of the LEA to the point where he made a special trip to London to plead with the national government (Department of Education and Science) to restore a proposed new elementary school to the building program. In reporting on both of the Sheffield protests, the *Times Educational Supplement* commented that "these parents, like many of their children, seem to have realized that in an over-bureaucratic age, the only thing to do is to raise one's voice."[27]

In 1969 the political parties began to take note of rising citizen protest over schools. The Labor Party talked of the need for a new education law, which should include better procedures for parents to appeal decisions made by school officials. The *Times Educational Supplement* reacted to such suggestions with the comment that there was little parent power before the comprehensive school movement and there was still very little parent power. In fact, said the *Times Educational Supplement,* parent power may be inconsistent with a national system of education.[28]

In June of that year the Labor Party came out in favor of

having parents (and teachers) appointed to the board of managers (or board of governors) of a school. The suggestion included a note of caution that this be tried on an experimental basis for awhile.[29]

The Conservative Party talked more about restoring power to the local governments, but in the fall of 1969 did suggest that any local plan for reorganizing schools which had the support of parents (and teachers) would meet with its approval.[30]

By June 1970, as the national elections neared, the Labor Party made a promise of promoting more parent (and teacher) participation in policy making if returned to office.

> One major aim will be to give more power to teachers and parents so that they can share the decisions made in schools for their children but on which at present they are never asked for their opinion. We want to improve the quality of participation in education.[31]

The upsurge of citizen protest and suggestions about giving parents some control over the schools alarmed the headmasters, and they took a public stand against what they called the "Frankenstein monster" of parent power. At the annual meeting of the National Association of Head Teachers in May 1969 a resolution was passed stressing that participation by parents could be harmful. Some of the speakers spoke of "good ideas getting out of hand" and of parents thinking they had a right to help run the school.[32]

The head of the Confederation for the Advancement of State Education responded to the stand taken by the head teachers by terming it "outrageous."

> What is outrageous... is that they are flying in the face of evidence which shows how important it is for parents to get involved.... One is almost pushed to saying that some of these heads who fear their schools being taken over possibly deserve it....[33]

The *Times Educational Supplement* also spoke out vigorously against the head teachers on the parent power question.

> The head teachers did themselves no good by hitting the headlines with a protest against "monster" parents and the spectre of parent power. It is easy enough to understand what they had in mind, but less easy to admire either their tactics or their appreciation of the stirrings which are now taking place. It will take more than a few heady platform speeches to obliterate the clear evidence that parents as well as teachers have much to contribute to a child's education. The only point of argument is how the cooperation between home and school can best be organized. Mr. Short [Secretary of the Department of Education and Science] and others like him think it needs to be institutionalized—through governing bodies and in other ways. He may well be right though this also means finding ways of making governing bodies more effective, which isn't easy. As for American experience, quoted with horror at Blackpool, it is not by any means as discouraging as some speakers seem to suppose.[34]

Letters to the editor tended to support the *Times Educational Supplement* in its editorial on the head teachers. The following is typical of such letters.

> Sir,—I would wholeheartedly wish to agree with your comments (May 30) regarding the emotional outbursts by head teachers at Blackpool.
> Today, the tide of cooperate responsibility for the education of young people seems to be rolling forward, and I would hope that, despite such outbursts, it will continue to do so. Teachers are in the privileged position of being allowed to freely practise their art upon the offspring of others. Surely, therefore, parents should be encouraged to participate actively in the educational process.[35]

Some of the letter writers reminded the head teachers that many parents were now better educated than the teachers.

Moreover, some of these parents were connected with the growing "knowledge industry" and were quite well informed on education.[36]

Apparently the head teachers were not the only ones bothered by parent or citizen participation. Many teachers doubted the wisdom of parental participation, and NUT took the line that any plans for parental participation should be initiated by the teachers. Not surprisingly, the organization representing citizen involvement, the Confederation for the Advancement of State Education (CASE), took issue with this point of view. CASE maintained that citizen groups had done quite well on their own, and, in fact, were responsible for such improvements as child art exhibits, book shows, getting LEAs to publish booklets describing the schools, and so on. In some of these activities CASE reported that it had encountered teacher resentment and opposition.[37]

In the 1970s parent and citizen protest continued, and at times came into open conflict with the aims of teachers. This occurred in Dulwich in 1970 when teachers went on strike and closed down the schools. A deputation of seventy angry mothers stormed the office of the chief education officer of the Inner London Education Authority and demanded that the schools be opened either by raising the teacher's pay or by hiring replacements for the striking teachers. The chief education officer replied by citing the power arrangements in England, namely that salaries are determined at the national level (by the Burnham Committee) and that he could not hire replacements for the striking teachers because it would arouse the ire of the teachers' associations.[38]

Continued failure to get satisfaction for citizen demands led to the suggestion that each LEA appoint an ombudsman to hear complaints by citizens against schools and teachers, but the LEAs spoke out against the concept.

Even well-organized parent groups found it difficult at times to achieve their objectives. This was the case in the Conservative Party stronghold of Richmond, one of the London boroughs and one of the eight LEAs which defied the national government Circular 10/65 calling for the reorganization of secondary education to provide for comprehensive schools. Parents in favor of comprehensive schools were organized, and at one point secured 12,000 signatures on a petition calling for comprehensive schools. But the system of separate grammar schools and selection at eleven-plus continued in Richmond because a majority of the voters voted for the Conservative Party candidates and their platform of maintaining the existing educational arrangements.[39]

Conservative Party parents and Labor Party parents were often in agreement, however, on the issue of parental rights in the choice of a school for their children. Until the late 1960s parents were not forced to send their children to the school nearest their home. As long as they could secure the permission of the headmaster, their children could enter the school of the parents' choice. As comprehensive schools were built, there was a growing tendency for the officials of the LEA to assign children to schools; in some cases the specific assignment ran counter to the wishes of the parents, and sometimes that of the headmaster.

In community after community where disputes arose over choice of school, parents organized and protested. In the case of South Benfleet, Essex, the parents conducted a seven-month fight to get their children into the school of their choice over the opposition of the LEA officials and the headmaster. The Confederation for the Advancement of State Education supported the parents in Essex and campaigned nationally for better legal procedures for the airing of parent grievances.[40]

CASE claimed that it did little good to contact the chief education officer and that letters to the national government from irate parent or citizen groups were answered only after intervals of several months. In July 1972 the Secretary of the Department of Education and Science reported that the number of complaints from parents against LEAs over the issue of choice of school was increasing. The previous school year there had been about 1000 such complaints reaching her office. She claimed that in a majority of cases the complaints were settled at the local level.[41]

In the case of the Inner London Education Authority the issue of parental choice of school was complicated by racial factors. The influx of "colored" immigrants had led to certain schools being filled predominately with "colored" students from Pakistan, the West Indies, and African countries. Under the system operating until 1972 parental choice of school resulted in some schools getting a disproportionate number of "high ability" children and other schools were loaded with the average and "low ability" children.

In 1972 the Inner London Education Authority announced a new system whereby the LEA would allocate children so that all schools would get their share of the "high ability" children, and of the "low ability" children. One member of the Education Committee of the Inner London Education Authority said that the new plan would cut down on discrimination against "colored" eleven-year-olds.[42] The plan was also defended by the LEA in terms of getting a good mix of intellectual abilities.

Hundreds of parents filed protests with the education officials of the Inner London Education Authority over the new plan.[43] The parallel with protests over attempts in the United States to achieve a balance racial mix by busing and reassignment of students is striking.

Under the London plan, both parents and headmasters lost control over the allocation of school children. The parents could no longer pick the school to apply to and the headmaster could no longer accept or reject an applicant.

Interestingly enough, the Confederation for the Advancement of State Education saw the choice of school issue as a false one. As early as 1969, CASE had taken the position that choice of school was not the main issue; instead, each parent should focus on improvement of the school where his child was.

Sir,—We naturally welcome the growing support of both educationists and politicians for the idea of increased parental involvement in education. . . .

The matter of choice of schools we feel to be something of a red herring. As you rightly pointed out it scarcely exists in practice, except for those who pay for independent education, and those who come high enough on the list of selected passes to gain their first choice school. We are far more anxious to raise the general standards within maintained schools to a level of excellence which would give parents little cause to want to send their children travelling great distances because of concern about the quality of their neighbourhood school. . . .

While we recognize that many parents need more help to enable them to understand the criteria for judging these things the question of quality is a more fundamental one than that of the provision of choice.

Maurice Plaskow
Chairman, Confederation for
the Advancement of State
Education.
1 Lakeside, Weybridge, Surrey.[44]

Some black leaders in the United States have taken a similar stance by arguing that getting their black children into a white school is less important than getting top quality education in the black schools.

The tough question is how can citizens exert pressure to insure good quality education in their children's schools? Citizens in England in the various LEAs tried repeatedly to apply such pressure. Sometimes the parents found a sympathetic LEA but to no avail because the purse strings for improvement of the school building and the classroom facilities are in the hands of the national government. This was the case in 1972 in Brighton where parents at four elementary schools kept their children home to dramatize the overcrowded and out-of-date facilities. The Education Committee of the LEA agreed with the parents, but the national government (Department of Education and Science) refused to allocate additional funds to Brighton to build new schools.[45]

In the case of Berkshire the parents were more successful. A local unit of CASE protested a proposed reduction of 85 teachers in the teaching staff to save money. Some 300 persons demonstrated outside the county government building. The teachers and the local Member of Parliament also protested and the plan was withdrawn.[46]

The examples of Brighton and Berkshire are fairly typical in that protesting parents trying to improve their schools through direct pressure lose as many battles as they win. There is another approach—an indirect one—where parent choice of school is supposed to generate improvement in the schools. A group of writers in the United States and Canada have called this the "voucher plan."

Under the voucher plan the local government (probably using federal government funds) would give the parents a check for a set amount to be used to pay for the tuition of their child at a school of their choice—public or private. Defenders of the plan argue that in the United States public schools have a near monopoly and that monopoly produces in school bureaucrats: a) indifferent attitudes; b) lack of response; c) authoritarian attitudes toward the "clients;" and d) complacency and a tendency to preserve the status quo.[47]

Two English educators (Frank Musgrove and Philip H. Taylor) have picked up the idea and modified it to meet the situation in England. They argue that there is oppressive control over curriculum and method by teachers in England which could be broken by giving parents complete freedom to choose their school, presumably one which represents a philosophy of education pleasing to them. They cite the private schools of England as evidence of how it would work and advocate that in the publicly-maintained schools parents be given complete free choice.[48]

Interestingly enough, many of the supporters of voucher

plans in the United States hope to secure a free or more open kind of education ("progressive education" is the old term) for the children, while in England some of the supporters of voucher-type plans are conservative people trying to avoid the progressivism of the county schools.

> As increases in taxation make it difficult for middle-class people to send their children to private schools, so the very rich become more priviledged. Yet, all parents need educational choice at the present time. As the state [national government] moves toward a system of uniform, neighborhood eomprehensives, the need for some alternatives, some freedom of movement, must grow. And it is profoundly important that parents should have the right to opt out of the pseudo-religion of progressivism, if they judge this a denial of their own beliefs, values, standards or way of life.[49]

Those supporting the voucher plan in the United States hope to make wide use of private schools. The idea is that by choosing this or that private school the parents will get the schools to offer what the parents want. In point of fact, it may not work that way at all. England has had a long experience with private schools, and the top 100 or so of these schools have high prestige and high academic quality. These top schools, however, are very much like each other, and hundreds of other private schools of lesser stature try faithfully to copy the top schools.

It turns out that the better the school is, the higher its prestige, the less control parents have over the school. Ian Weinberg studied these top schools and found that the headmasters are very powerful and keep the parents at a distance to protect the teachers from interference.[50]

Weinberg also found that in these top private schools the parents do not form parent-teacher associations, or any other type of association, which might be a vehicle for transmitting their views to the school authorities. Moreover, the parents really don't know what is going on in the schools because the children board at the school. Even on visiting days they learn very little because the schools encourage the tradition that the student doesn't "squeal"—on the school or on his fellow students. These top schools usually have plenty of applicants and they choose the parents as much as the parents choose the school.

In the publicly-maintained schools in England freedom of choice for parents would run into difficulties such as the social class barriers which make working-class parents timid and deferential in the presence of the kind of people who serve on the governing boards of schools. Other difficulties include the tradition of classroom autonomy for the teacher, the tradition of strong headmasters, and the high prestige of the grammar school which makes even a middle-class parent so grateful when his child gets into one that he is not about to quarrel with what the school teaches or how it teaches.

There are a very small number of "progressive" parents—with money—in England who send their children to experimental private schools which remind one of the fly-by-night "free schools" in the United States. Typically, these schools are very small, rather short on money and facilities, and show no signs of competing successfully with the hundreds of traditional private schools (which enroll about 6 percent of school-age children) or with the publicly-maintained system which enrolls close to 94 percent of the school children. Weinberg contends that these "progressive"-type parents would probably cause trouble if their children were enrolled in one of the famous private schools.[51]

RIGHT-WING REACTION

One of the curious side effects of the outpouring of citizenprotest in England is that it has encouraged persons to speak out who don't believe in educational equality or in educational methods based on allowing freedom for young pupils. Some of these persons openly identify themselves as elitists, while others stress the fixed nature of the intelligence quotient (IQ) and what they see as a fact of life, namely that some people have high intellectual ability. Some of these right-wing critics are lay persons, but many are educators, frequently university professors or teachers and headmasters from the academic secondary school (grammar school). There are even some conservative head teachers from the elementary schools. The more sensational of the criticisms have appeared in print as "Black Papers."

One is reminded of the outburst of criticism against "progressive education" in the 1950s in the United States, led by a mixed bag of liberal arts professors in colleges and journalists catering to right-wing audiences and to all those persons who thought we were coddling our youth.

In England the "Black Papers" and the like surfaced after the controversy over comprehensive secondary schools versus separate grammar schools had reached a fever pitch after much publicizing, especially in the United States, of England's progressive elementary schools which featured freedom, openness, and choice for the young children. In addition, several years of rapidly growing enrollments in higher education had caused one group of professors to complain about lowered standards, changed atmosphere, and so on. Novelist Kingsley Amis was one of these critics and was credited with the phrase that in higher education "more means worse."

The first set of "Black Papers" appeared in 1969 under the title *Fight for Education,* and in nine months had sold 25,000 copies. The second set of "Black Papers" was published in October 1969, and the third in November 1970. All three were then brought together and published under one cover. By 1971 about 80,000 copies of the "Black Papers" had been sold.

The criticisms focused on the new methods in elementary schools, the comprehensive schools and the danger they posed to the high standards of academic education, and the harmful effects of the expansion of enrollments in higher education. Reference was made to the United States and the defects of its educational system.[52]

The "Black Papers" generated much discussion. Supporters of the old-fashioned, tough education were encouraged to speak out. At a meeting of a subunit of the LEA in South Dorset a town councilman asserted that children left school (at age fifteen) in a state of illiteracy. He felt schools should get down to the basics and teach the "3 r's." The manager of a factory spoke up to say that in selecting apprentices, ages fifteen to seventeen, he found more than half of the applicants unable to do simple arithmetic problems. A former chairman of the Education Committee asserted that illiteracy had increased in the last ten years.[53]

Many spoke out in opposition to the conservative views represented by the "Black Papers." Note was taken of the fact that some of the professors writing essays in criticism of elementary school teaching were themselves under attack by their university students for bad teaching.

> Sir,—It is encouraging to find, in *Black Papers and Perspectives,* so many well-known people have begun to study the work of the primary school.
> (We must assume, of course, that these writers have undertaken study, since, in the academic tradition they so much admire, this would be prerequisite for publication.) It is particularly gratifying that they are prepared to give the time to this at a moment when they are so much under fire from their own students, and from some sections of the general public, but they are undoubtedly right to look for the causes of their dissatisfaction in early education. The historical and statistical evidence on the proportion of present students and staff who have had any primary education other than that of a traditional kind would prove a useful appendix to either book....[54]

The "Black Paper" writers were characterized as "a pessimistic alliance of elitists for whom education has become the focus of all anxiety and Law, Order and Patriotism."[55]

The national government took alarm at the mounting right-wing criticism, and the head of the Department of Education and Science in April 1969 made a speech at a meeting of the National Union of Teachers denouncing what he called the flood of reaction which threatened the content, methods and organization of education developed over the past ten years. He wondered whether the criticism had been triggered by a reaction to the extremist actions of a small number of university student protesters but then went on to link the "Black Papers" with a massive movement toward reaction, including "reaction of racism, of demands for capital and corporal punishment, of the ending of the welfare state and now of reaction in education." [56] He appealed for unity in the teaching profession to meet the threat.

> The philosophy of the "Black Paper" threatens the achievements of a generation and the threat must be met by every teacher throughout the country and by the great teachers' organizations nationally.[57]

Defenders of the "Black Paper" point of view reacted quickly to the speech of the Secretary of the Department of Education and Science (Edward Short). The following letter to the *Times Educational Supplement* was typical of the defenders.

> Sir,—I write to protest about Mr. Short's speech to the N.U.T.
> If it was intended to take the minds of his audience off the meagreness of their pay packet I suppose it achieved some success. If it was meant to be informative to parents, and others interested in education, it was the most dangerous piece of double think ever spoken by a Minister of Education and had a real 1984 ring about it.
> As an educational writer to magazines I receive a large number of letters from parents worried about problems of schooling. Why can't Johnny read at eight or Marilyn at eleven plus or worse still, why is Bill at fourteen still illiterate? Why can't Susan do math? We can't talk to George's teacher—he always squashes us. Do you think a class of 42 is too big? We don't want to send Mary to the

comprehensive in the next street because the children who go are ill mannered and untidy. . . .

It would seem from this flow of letters that the schools cannot cope adequately with parents worries and it seems ludicrous that the job should be done by the women's magazines. The parents are generally worried by the things the Black Paper sought to remedy. They complain of the discipline being too permissive, of a fall in standards in reading and mathematics in primary schools, of second-class education given by the comprehensives and lack of choice of school. Mr. Short would do well to realize that these are the worries of the ordinary parent and not merely the views of the eminent men like C. P. Snow whom he castigates so roundly as reactionary.

Mr. Short describes the Black Paper as the worst thing that has happened to education in 100 years. Have all his predecessors also been asleep in their ivory towers at Curzon Street? Is no one allowed to disagree with him educationally? Is the Department of Education taking over the role of George Orwell's Ministry of Love with Mr. Short as Big Brother—or could he be just Rip Van Winkle?[58]

Criticism of progressive methods has continued in England and has zeroed in on what is called a widespread inability of the English child to read efficiently and to understand what he has read. In 1972, after much pressure from citizens and educators alike, the national government stepped in and appointed a national commission to investigate the teaching of reading.

Citizen Militancy

Leaving aside the "Black Paper" types as extremists, parent and citizen discontent in England in the 1970s seems more vigorous than that in the United States, if we leave aside the issue of busing for racial balance. Even if the busing issue is included, the protest in England is more striking, if for no other reason than that England historically is not a country dedicated to the proposition of "schools serving the people."

In community after community, English parents protest the failure of the county authorities to eliminate the harsh selection procedure called the "eleven-plus" or the failure to build comprehensive secondary schools. Other kinds of parents lucky enough to have a child in the elite grammar school fight any proposal to close the grammar school and merge with a comprehensive school. Parents demonstrate in front of the city hall, withhold their children from school, contact their LEA officials, and sign petitions and letters by the thousands which are sent to the ultimate source of power—the national government.

These protests occur in large communities and in small ones, in rural areas and in urban ones. Examples abound, and the following are cited as illustrative. In 1971 parents at the Vauxhall Manor School, South London, threatened to withdraw their children unless the Inner London Education Authority provided a new building (the teachers also threatened to resign unless there was a new building). [59] In two Hertfordshire towns (Hertford and Ware) parents mounted a campaign to end the eleven-plus selection immediately even though the LEA was moving gradually toward a fully comprehensive system by 1975. [60] In Buckinghamshire 21,000 people signed a petition against selection and in favor of comprehensive secondary schools. [61]

Some of the citizen protest was coordinated by the Confederation for the Advancement of State Education. In addition to helping out in this or that community where there is citizen discontent, CASE also has campaigned nationally on specific issues. Thus, in 1971 and 1972 CASE sought to mobilize support for the proposal to raise the school leaving age to sixteen because there was much apathy and some opposition to the proposal. CASE also publicly criticized the concept of LEAs trying to avoid tax increases by cutting the number of teachers and increasing the number of pupils assigned to a teacher.

Other citizen organizations have formed in response to a specific issue. This was the case at the end of the 1960s with the drive to provide more nursery schools and/or playground facilities for the three and four-year-olds. All of the five-year-olds in England are in school because that is the age compulsory school attendance begins, but well into the 1960s England had less than 10 percent of its three- and four-year olds in nursery school—one of the worst records in Western Europe and even below that of the United States.

Citizens organized into the Pre-School Playgroups Association and were increasingly successful in their lobbying for more facilities for young children. As the *Times Educational Supplement* put it, the Pre-School Playgroups Association knows where the power lies and has applied pressure to Westminister (Parliament).[62]

In 1972, the "lollypop lobby," as these supporters of nursery schools and playground groups were called, brought hundreds of mothers to visit Members of Parliament and to pressure for more emphasis on nursery-age education. They also fired off petitions to the Department of Education and Science calling for more money for nursery education and for continuation of an urban aid program whereby playgrounds and nursery schools were funded as part of an urban renewal program.[63]

As nursery schools and playground groups enroll more and more three- and four-year-olds, sentiment has developed in favor of involving mothers in the actual operation of these groups. In one sense this is just a continuation of the Plowden Report idea of involving parents to inform them of what the school is doing. There is also the thought that the experiences will enable the mother to return home and upgrade the educational quality of the home environment. There are even a few educators, such as Brian Jackson, who see parental participation as an opportunity to bring democracy into the operation of early childhood education. Others, however, doubt whether mothers will fit in and be able to help. Some persons are also concerned that it will end up being a case of cheap labor being used to replace professional teachers.

The United States has experienced a similar interest in the care and education of children under the age of five. The Headstart Program generated some early optimism and then some disillusionment as it sought to prepare young children for the school experience that would come later (at age six). There was much talk about compensating for the deficiencies of the home environment. The Headstart Program was supposed to involve low-income parents in the running of the program, but civil rights groups and other liberals complained that governmental authorities at the local level were often reluctant to involve parents in this way.

In the 1970s the day care programs attracted much attention as a way to free the mother in a low-income family so that she could work. Much of the enthusiasm and support for these programs came from middle-class women who wished to be relieved of some of the child-rearing responsibilities so that they could work full-time. The extremist among these women (usually upper-middle-class, white women) spoke of the "liberation" of women. A bill to provide a large-scale program of day care centers financed by federal funds passed Congress but was vetoed by President Nixon in November 1971. The cost of the program may have been a factor in the presidential veto, but there was also concern among conservatives over a feature of the bill which gave considerable control over the program to parents instead of to local and state government officials. Under the bill each day care center would have been controlled by a ten-man council; half of the members of the council would be parents and the other half would be selected from the local community but must meet the approval of the five parents on the council.

Precedents for parent and citizen participation had been set by the Elementary-Secondary Education Act of 1965. Title I of the Act, to help school children from low-income families, required that each local school district appoint a council of citizens to advise on educational policy. Many districts failed to appoint these councils, or appointed persons not representative of the low income area, or failed to make use of these councils after they were appointed.

England has its own program to improve schools and community life in low-income areas. These are called Educational Priority Areas (EPA), and in the spring of 1972 involved 570 schools. Each teacher in these schools was paid £75 extra (about $180), and there were special national government grants for school buildings in these areas.

The head of the EPA program, sociologist A. H. Halsey, is one of the few in England to stress citizen participation as a way to improve schools and upgrade communities. Maurice Kogan, professor of social science, is another as he asserts that "participation is indeed the largest single issue facing the British Welfare State in the 1970s." [64] It is much more common in England to talk about revitalizing the local government in somewhat traditional terms.

Halsey's rhetoric reminds one of the community control advocates in the Oceanhill-Brownsville dispute in New York City in 1968 and 1969 where black parents sought to gain control over their schools. Speaking in the spring of 1972, Halsey said that it is more important to improve the parent's capacity to teach than to improve the teacher's capacity to teach. England, he said, must go beyond the Plowden Report concept of parental involvement and think of parental participation as involving the revitalization of whole communities. He added that all of this (parental involvement and EPA programs) won't be enough "without tackling the maldistribution of wealth and power which dog our society." [65] This last point was echoed in the fall of 1972 by Christopher

Jencks. After a study of American schools and attempts to integrate racially, he claimed that changing schools won't produce equality. Rather, we have to redistribute income, guarantee good housing, and so on. [66] The clear implication is that all of this would be done by vigorous government action at the national level. England has had considerable experience with strong actions by the national government in the field of education, but only very brief experience with ordinary citizens having some control over their schools.

The Future for Citizen Participation

Even though parent and citizen protest about school issues is vigorous in England, some educators continue to assert that citizen or parent power is not an important factor.

> But in general in English education today, what is still remarkable is not the power of clients (whether pupils or their parents), but their impotence.[67]

These same educators claim that parent-teacher associations have not gotten off the ground.[68]

It has also been asserted that parental and community pressure did not produce the recent innovations in England's elementary schools. Rather it was the work of enlightened professionals. [69] The failure of similar reforms to spread more quickly in the United States has been attributed to parental and community pressure in favor of continuance of a hardline, academic type of education which the post-Sputnik era fostered.[70]

Stuart Maclure, editor of the *Times Educational Supplement*, argued that it is difficult for the "consumers" to bring pressure to bear on the national government to influence educational policy. He also expressed doubt that the Confederation for the Advancement of State Education would ever be effective.[71]

These are pessimistic views, but it is possible that the long-range effects of citizen participation have not yet been fully understood in England. Partly this may be because England has nothing as dramatic as the annual turnout of voters in a school district in the United States to vote for or against candidates for the school board on the basis of their "liberal" or "conservative" views on education, or to vote for or against a bond issue to raise funds for new school buildings, facilities, and programs. In these ways dissatisfaction with school policy can be expressed. In 1971-72, when anger against busing of children to achieve racial balance reached a fever pitch, less than half of these school bond issues passed. One of the more notorious cases occurred in Detroit when voters refused to vote funds fot the schools even though the city was under a court order to bus children and needed to buy hundreds of buses for that purpose.

There are some in the United States who argue that citizen participation harms the quality of education. Cohen, in 1969, put it negatively by saying that research failed to indicate that citizen participation in black neighborhoods improved the achievement levels of black children.[72] In the same year Theodore Sizer, Dean of Harvard University's School of Education, asserted that the quality of education would improve with community control of education.[73] Yet, in New York City, after three years of citizen participation in a system of 31 decentralized school districts, the head of the entire school system reported that there was little evidence to indicate that pupil achievement levels had gone up.[74]

It has also been suggested that when school boards in the United States attempt to please, or placate, any group in society—including the majority group—education in the schools suffers. The curriculum is then limited to those things which everyone endorses, and teachers tend to be selected on the basis of colorlessness and inoffensive life style. Thus, the student is stiffled in his attempt to explore and develop autonomy and maturity.[75]

It has been pointed out, however, that most parents don't criticize the school, and of those who do only a small fraction take any kind of steps to press for action.[76]

Yet many educational leaders in the United States believe in citizen control over education and suggest that this can be achieved best by breaking big school districts into smaller ones, closer to the people. Thus, New York City with one school board for over 8 million people, now has 31 school districts with school boards, though the central school board still exists and retains more power than the reformers had wished. England, in contrast, is seeking to revitalize local government by substituting 93 larger units for the existing 145 LEAs.

The battle over integration of schools in the United States has been a factor in promoting citizen control. Some of the civil rights leaders favor breaking schools loose from the control of city or county authorities and establishing, instead, neighborhood school boards controlled by people of the neighborhood. These are often neighborhoods of Black people, and lower-class people at that. There is no counterpart in England of this attempt to establish machinery for involvement of working-class people on a large scale, though working-class parents have protested about school issues— witness the Sheffield example.

Americans of a liberal persuasion cite a number of potential benefits from citizen participation in the control of public schools. First of all, in the case of Black neighborhoods, quality education replaces Black Power as a slogan. Secondly, in any neighborhood, Black or white, parents begin to learn more about the educational process and the home becomes a better environment for learning. Third, a sense of community develops which then leads to more public support of public schools. Fourth, with community control there is increased willingness of schools to experiment and innovate, particularly with regard to the needs of ethnic minorities. Finally, participation is cited as a worthy end in itself. The overall effect is that parents gain a bit of control over their child's destiny, and teachers view citizens as allies and as resources to draw upon, rather than as roadblocks.

Some of the leaders of the teachers' organizations in the United States, but probably not a majority, favor a measure of citizen control over education. They see such lay participation by lower-class citizens as a weapon to upset the traditional control over education by middle-class school boards and the middle-class citizens they chiefly represent. It is argued that educational change is unlikely as long as the citadel of opposition remains unchallenged. Included in the opponents of change are people who value low taxes more than education and those oriented toward the values of business and industry. School administrators (principals and superintendents of schools) are included in the opposition and the claim is that teacher power will never equal or exceed that of the administrator unless they have ordinary citizens as their allies.[77]

The use of citizens as allies can be a two-edged sword since experience in some American cities shows citizen groups denouncing teachers on strike, and even assaulting them physically. These have usually been situations where the teachers were white and the parents Black and where racial feelings had gotten out of hand.

Participation by citizens in the control of schools, in either England or the United States, probably increases their valuation of education as important and, in the case of lower-class people especially, heightens their educational aspirations for their children. It also tends to make citizens critical of their schools.

England and the United States seem to be moving toward

each other as the isolation of the teacher in England from community pressure begins to end while teachers in the United States, long subject to community pressure, militantly seek to assert a measure of autonomy for the professional.[78]

NOTES

1. C. A. Bowers, Ian Housego and Doris Dyke, eds., *Education and Social Policy: Local Control of Education.* New York: Random House, 1970, pp. 14-15.
2. Eric Hoffer, *The Temper of Our Times.* New York: Harper and Row, 1967, p. 44.
3. H. C. Dent, *The Educational System of England and Wales.* London: Univ. of London Press, 1961, p. 211.
4. A description of this period is found in Lawrence A. Cremin, *The Transformation of the School.* New York: Random House, 1961, pp. 328-353.
5. George Baron, "The Pattern of Administration and the Curriculum-UK" *Yearbook of Education, 1958.* Yonkers-on-Hudson, N.Y.: World, 1958, p. 359.
6. Muriel Beadle, *These Ruins Are Inhabited.* New York: Doubleday, 1961, p. 297.
7. Robin Pedley, *The Comprehensive School.* London: Pelican, 1963, p. 11.
8. Frank Musgrove and Philip H. Taylor, *Society and the Teacher's Role.* London: Routledge and Kegan Paul, 1969, p. 1.
9. Ibid., p. 4.
10. Dent, op. cit., p. 212.
11. Times Educational Supplement (London), January 31, 1964, p. 237.
12. A. D. C. Peterson, "Educational Reform in England and Wales, 1955-1966." Comparative Education Review, Vol. XI, No. 3, Oct. 1967, p. 289.
13. Times Educational Supplement (London), October 12, 1962, p. 443.
14. Richard Batley, Oswald O'Brien, and Henry Parris, *Going Comprehensive: Educational Policy-Making in Two County Boroughs.* London: Routledge and Kegan Paul, 1970, pp. 2, 11-12, 89-93.
15. Central Advisory Council for Education (England). *Children and*

their *Primary Schools,* Vol. I. London: Her Majesty's Stationery Office, 1967, pp. 37-49.
  16. Ibid., p. 39.
  17. Robert J. Fisher, *Learning How to Learn: The English Primary School and American Education.* New York: Harcourt, Brace and Jovanovich, 1972, pp. 8-9.
  18. Department of Education and Science, *Parent-Teacher Relations in Primary Schools.* London: Her Majesty's Stationery Office, 1968, p. 48.
  19. Frederick M. Wirt and Michael W. Kirst, *The Political Web of American Schools.* Boston: Little, Brown, 1972, p. 53.
  20. *Children and their Primary Schools,* op. cit., pp. 37-38.
  21. For an analysis of the American educator's identification with the values and techniques of the business world, see Raymond E. Callahan, *Education and the Cult of Efficiency.* Chicago: Univ. of Chicago Press, 1962.
  22. Brian Jackson and Dennis Marsden, *Education and the Working Class.* London: Routledge and Kegan Paul, 1962, pp. 116-117.
  23. *Parent-Teacher Relations,* op. cit., p. 40.
  24: Ibid., p. 38.
  25. Times Educational Supplement (London), June 21, 1968, p. 2054.
  26. Ibid., March 7, 1969, p. 733.
  27. Ibid., May 9, 1969, p. 1542.
  28. Ibid., March 28, 1969, p. 985.
  29. Ibid., June 30, 1969, p. 2023.
  30. Ibid., Sept. 12, 1969, p. 28.
  31. Ibid., June 12, 1970, p. 2.
  32. Ibid., May 30, 1969, p. 1792.
  33. Ibid.
  34. Ibid., p. 1761.
  35. Ibid., June 13, 1969, p. 1955.
  36. Ibid., June 6, 1969, p. 1874.
  37. Ibid., June 20, 1969, p. 2047.
  38. Ibid., Feb. 6, 1970, p. 6.
  39. Ibid., June 5, 1970, p. 2.
  40. Ibid., April 21, 1972, p. 3.
  41. Ibid., July 21, 1972, p. 10.
  42. Ibid., June 30, 1972, p. 5.
  43. Ibid.
  44. Ibid., April 11, 1969, p. 1180.
  45. Ibid., April 21, 1972, p. 8.

46. Ibid., June 23, 1972, p. 8.
47. Lawrence W. Downey, "The Struggle for Control of Education" p. 94 in C. A. Bowers, et. al., op. cit.
48. Musgrove and Taylor, op. cit., pp. 85-86.
49. C. B. Cox and A. E. Dyson, *The Black Papers on Education*. London: Davis-Poynter, 1971, p. 32.
50. Ian Weinberg, *The English Public School: The Sociology of Elite Education*. New York: Atherton, 1967, pp. 61, 154.
51. Ibid., p. 158.
52. C. B. Cox and A. E. Dyson, *The Black Papers on Education*. London: David-Poynter, 1971, pp. 31, 138-150.
53. Times Educational Supplement (London), April 11, 1969, p. 1183.
54. Ibid., May 23, 1969, p. 1726.
55. Anthony Sampson, *The New Anatomy of Britain*. New York: Stein and Day, 1972, p. 126.
56. Times Educational Supplement (London), April 11, 1969, p. 1168.
57. Ibid.
58. Ibid., April 18, 1969, p. 1257.
59. Ibid., May 14, 1971, p. 5.
60. Ibid., May 14, 1971, p. 11.
61. Ibid., June 21, 1972, p. 10.
62. Ibid., May 16, 1969, p. 1585.
63. Ibid., April 14, 1972, p. 5.
64. Maurice Kogan, *The Government of Education*. New York: Citation, 1971, p. 40.
65. Times Educational Supplement (London), April 14, 1972, p. 10.
66. Christopher Jencks and Mary Jo Bane, "Schools and Inequality." Washington Post, Sept. 17, 1972. Outlook section.
67. Musgrove and Taylor, op. cit., p. 11.
68. Ibid.
69. Michael Katz in Kogan, op. cit., p. 9.
70. Vincent R. Rogers, ed., *Teaching in the British Primary School*. New York: Macmillan, 1970, pp. 290-291.
71. History of Education Society (England), *Studies in the Government and Control of Education Since 1860*. London: Methuen, 1970, p. 3.
72. David K. Cohen, "The Price of Community Control," Commentary, Vol. 48, July 1969, p. 28; also cited in Bowers, et. al., op. cit., p. 40.

73. Theodore R. Sizer, "The Case for a Free Market." Saturday Review, Jan. 11, 1969, pp. 34 ff.
74. Bernard Bard, "Is Decentralization Working?" Phi Delta Kappan. Vol. LIV, No. 4, Dec. 1972, p. 240.
75. Bowers, et. al., op. cit., p. 16.
76. Wirt and Kirst, op. cit., pp. 91-92.
77. Stephen Zeluck, "The UFT: Will it Destroy the AFT?" Phi Delta Kappan, Vol. L, No. 5, Jan. 1969, pp. 250-254.
78. R. K. Kelsall and H. M. Kelsall, "The Status, Role and Future of Teachers," pp. 129-130 in Edmund J. King, ed., *The Teacher and the Needs of Society in Evolution*. New York: Pergamon, 1970.

Chapter 8

CONCLUSIONS

It is important for both Americans and Englishmen to understand the ramifications of growing national power in the field of education. England's experience with this phenomenon in the 1960s and 1970s suggests the following generalizations:

> *1. Individual freedom and personal choice have been reduced for some individuals, for some groups, and for some institutions.*

Thus, the intellectual elite no longer finds it as easy to segregate themselves from ordinary people in the process of getting a good academic education. Status-minded people, especially those with money, circumvent the system of controls in the public school system and buy a place for their child in the small private school system, which insures considerable social advantage, plus economic advantage later in the world of work. The private schools enroll about 6 percent of school age children.

Schools receiving public funds are no longer able to think of themselves as autonomous institutions relatively free to make decisions. Headmasters are no longer as free to reject the applications of parents for a place for their children, nor is the headmaster free to rule his teachers with an iron hand as before. The headmaster is now subject to a network of bureaucratic regulations issued by the national government and by the local governments. The local governments, in turn, are no longer free to hire as many teachers as they wish, or to build a school when or where they want, or to determine the pay of teachers. There are even signs that the national government is beginning to take a hand in determining which teachers will be dismissed from service.

Even the autonomous universities are no longer free to remain isolated centers of learning and eccentric behavior patronized mainly by upper-middle-class students. In 1964 the universities were brought under the jurisdiction of the national government's Ministry of Education which changed its name to Department of Education and Science. Since then fears have mounted in regard to subtle pressures on the universities by the national government.

Government restrictions, of course, can also work to enlarge freedom and opportunity for persons, especially those at the bottom of the social heap.

> 2. *Educational opportunity has been increased for those at the bottom, the so-called working-class.*

Examinations no longer eliminate 75 percent of the children at age eleven and assign them to secondary schools of low prestige. Such examinations still are used by some counties, but the national government is pressuring all counties to establish comprehensive secondary schools which will accept all children. Where separate academic secondary schools still exist they now accept an increasing number of students from working-class families. Such students, however, drop out of secondary schools in disproportionately high numbers. Universities also accept more working-class students, though they are underrepresented and they constitute a minority of all university students.

> 3. *A nationwide commitment to an equitable division of the nation's resources has been made, but the national government has not been able to solve the problems of status and social class differences which divide Englishmen almost as effectively as Negro-white differences do in the United States.*

Schools continue to be used as a weapon to confirm the status of ruling groups and to impress a sense of unworthiness on working-class children. In England, as in the United States, some school districts have a larger percentage of working-class families and less property to tax for the support of schools than do other districts (40 percent of the money for schools come from local taxes and 60 percent from the national government). The national government has tried to reduce the inequality between school districts (Local Education Authorities) by a series of actions which began in 1958 with the setting of a quota of teachers which each district could hire. In effect this meant that all districts would have their share of overcrowded classes rather than concentrating them in the slum areas of cities.

In England, as in the United States, conservatives have reacted to the various efforts to equalize by deploring such attempts as "leveling" and "social engineering." Conservatives tend to associate local autonomy with preservation of individual freedom, while the national government is characterized as distant and controlled by insensitive bureaucrats or politicians unresponsive to local needs.

> 4. *Central control does not inhibit innovation and reform in education.*

The indications are that many of the innovations and reforms in education in the last decade or so have been instigated by the national government, or by groups which used the power of the national government to implement their proposals. Notable exceptions are the "open" or progressive elementary schools and comprehensive schools prior to 1965. It is also apparent that some of the changes have been for the worse. For example, it was the national government in 1960 which curtailed the expansion of nursery school enrollment and left England unprepared to meet the new emphasis on the early years of childhood.

> 5. *The growing power of the national government has stimulated the growth of militancy among teachers and their organizations.*

The steady growth of professionalism among teachers seems to be threatened by national government actions of entering such areas as curriculum and salary determination formerly reserved to teachers and local governments. Strikes by teachers are one of several indications that teachers are determined to maintain—and even extend—their professional autonomy.

Being professional usually involves specialization—digging so deeply into a field that no one else, except your fellow professionals, knows what you are doing. A former United States Commissioner of Education, Harold Howe, has argued that with professionalization, as with everything else in a democracy, there must be a system of checks and balances—some procedure that is to keep the professionals responsive to the need of citizens.

> The professional, left unchecked, is liable to become a dictator; a school superintendent is no more exempt from becoming a hometown Hitler than the most pompous and arrogant Babbit whoever headed a school board.[1]

Professionalism has bumped into an outbreak of grassroots democracy—i.e., citizen protest.

6. *The growing power of the national government has stimulated an outburst of citizen protest indicating they want to be included in the decision-making process.*

Parents and other lay persons are demanding the right to choose the school their children will attend; the right to have comprehensive schools in some areas, and in other areas the right to continue having selective secondary schools (grammar schools); the right to have uncrowded classrooms for their children; and so on.

7. *Thanks to the national government, attention has shifted from the quality of education to such matters as balancing budgets, saving money, being more "productive," and building a strong national economy.*

The national government has begun to listen to the economists who think of "inputs" and "outputs" rather than human beings, and who see the educational enterprise as a production line to be made more efficient and thus able to turn out more units at less cost to the national economy. Such actions are in keeping with a trend in Western Europe toward educational planning as part of a national plan for economic development. The original impetus for such efforts in Europe was partly a desire to have the combined economic power of Western Europe be at least equal to that of the Soviet Union, and partly a desire to achieve economic strength sufficient to slow down the American takeover of European businesses.

8. *The movement toward growing national control of education has been encouraged inadvertently by teachers' organizations, citizen groups and local governments alike.*

As each group asks the national government to intervene it hopes that the particular issue will be decided in its favor, and sometimes it is. At the same time, however, the right of the national government to intervene has been established. It is not unknown for the national government then to enter into subsequent disputes on its own. The determination of teachers' salaries is a case in point.

A number of factors slow down or moderate the trend toward growing central power in England. For example, there are at least three traditions still alive in varying degrees which inhibit centralization: a) local control; b) academic freedom; and c) "muddling through."

Local control in education exists up to a point, and it is a rallying cry for those who would oppose a particular measure planned by the national government. The Department of Education and Science itself finds it convenient to cite local control when it wishes to avoid a request for intervention.

Academic freedom extends to teachers in elementary and secondary schools, as well as to those in higher education. In essence it means that there are limits beyond which no government should go in interfering with what a teacher does in his own classroom.

To a considerable extent the freedom enjoyed by teachers is an outgrowth of the English tradition of "muddling through," and the government does a minimum of planning and checking and hopes that everything will turn out all right. This inevitably leads to a moderate amount of inefficiency which again mitigates some of the control exercised from the top.

Part of the inefficiency stems from another tradition, that of practicality. As the English see it, you don't scrap something which you have. This plays havoc with central plans to build new patterns or new organizations in the field of education. This is largely the basis on which the church schools were retained as a part of England's system of "publicly supported" schools. The churches, in turn, have watched the national government very closely for fear that the church schools might be abolished or downgraded, as was the case under liberal regimes in France.

Conclusions

Centralization in education may have been slowed some by failures in central control in areas outside education, notably nationalization of the coal and steel industries.

Moreover, the national government in England is not free to act irresponsibly. The Secretary of the Department of Education and Science reports regularly to Parliament and on numerous occasions has to prepare careful answers to questions posed by members of Parliament. The questions and answers are widely published in the newspapers, especially in the *Times Educational Supplement.*

A major force against centralized control of education is the diversity that still remains among the Local Education Authorities. Attempts by the national government to eliminate the diversity tend to produce a reaction against centralization. This occurred at the end of the 1960s as the national government tried to whip the remaining 22 uncooperative LEAs into line on the comprehensive school issue.

Yet, local control over education in England is diminishing. But then England never really endorsed the concept of local control of education in the way Americans did. There was a 32-year period of experimentation with local school districts, but this ended in 1902 because the vigorous display of partisan interests over school board elections and educational policy frightened the ruling classes. In addition, the competition from the new public schools was a bit more than the church schools could tolerate. So in the interest of "social stability" larger educational units, coinciding with the county boundaries, were established. A big point was made at the time about larger units being more efficient but, in fact, vigorous neighborhood democracy was a bit unsettling to the "establishment."

Local control of education has now come to have little meaning in England. So many of the important issues are decided by the national government, either on its own or in consultation with the powerful teachers' organizations.

Of those matters not determined by the national government most are decided not by local governments but by the headmaster. His power has been eroded some, but he still runs his school in a firm manner which most American school principals would envy.

The teachers' organizations are challenging the headmasters on many matters, such as assignment to duties out of class, and have been successful in raising the whole issue of whether the head has unlimited power within his school.

Teachers' organizations have also kept a close watch on the national government, especially to insure that the tradition of negotiation be honored in any important educational change proposed. At the same time, the teachers' organizations have encouraged the national government to intervene on a number of issues.

In one sense it is natural that big teachers' organizations, notably the National Union of Teachers, encourage participation by the national government since a national teachers' organization can deal more efficiently with one national body than with a host of local government units.

At the same time a strong posture by the national government stimulates the teachers' groups to be aggressive. Lieberman recognized this as early as 1960 in commenting on the American scene.

> Centralization will dramatize the weakness of teachers' organizations and put into motion the forces that will eliminate these weaknesses.[2]

Aggressive central control in England has generated teacher militancy. Yet militancy may be a sign of teacher weakness rather than strength; it suggests an inability to influence educational change and professional development by the use of the normal channels. Then, too, militancy is probably confined to a minority of teachers. Most teachers are controlled subtly by their middle-class origins and by the training which society insists they must have before becoming a teacher. There is little evidence in either England or the United States that such training is designed to produce independent-minded professionals who are desirous, and capable, of participating in the running of the educational enterprise.

Most of England's teachers are trained in small, paternalistic institutions where the young prospective teachers are closely supervised. Only in the latter half of the 1960s did nineteen-year-old students in these training colleges protest against such rules as the one requiring girls to be in their rooms by 10 p.m. Thus, it is not surprising to find some English educators at the end of the 1960s saying that "the staff room [where teachers gather in their free time] is probably one of the most potent forces for conservatism in English education."[3]

A few years earlier that same staff room (common-room) was seen as a source of educational innovations and as an antidote to the growing power of the national government.

> There is a real commerce of thought throughout the teaching world; and as this doctrine or that circulates from one common-room to another, it is either rejected on its merits or woven into the fabric of our educational technique. Advance in this country has always come by dicussion in this way and never by superimposed direction; and if there is reason to believe that we shall be successful in adjusting our education to the requirements of a rapidly changing world, it is because there is this freedom in our schools, and within our common-rooms much lively discussion based on hard thinking.[4]

The above quote may apply more to grammar schools than to elementary schools, or to secondary modern schools. Moreover, individual teachers in both England and the United States increasingly rely on organizations which speak for them. Many benefits are gained by this procedure but any sense of personal power or involvement is reduced to a minimum. Perhaps the one job still retaining a sense of personal power is that of the headmaster, or head teacher, in England. But even the headmaster's days may be numbered as power is reallocated in the changing educational scene in England.

In the long run the greatest challenge to the headmaster's power may come from an aroused citizenry. The heavy hand of both the national government and the headmaster, along with the indecisiveness and powerlessness of the chief education officer of the LEA, have instigated neighborhood democracy in ways unintended. Thus, citizens in England are speaking out in a way which Americans have long been accustomed to but which in England is very "un-English." At the present time such citizen protest is largely confined to the middle class. Nonetheless, teachers in both England and the United States can no longer count on parental or citizen indifference.

It is difficult for teachers in England to accept citizens as a new member of the partnership which controls education. It should be easier for teachers in the United States because of the age-old ideology of schools serving the people. In truth, however, most of the teachers in the United States probably don't believe in lay control of education, that is in real situations as distinct from educational and political theory. [5] For them lay control conflicts with the professionalization of teaching and of school administration. Teachers have long favored a school system free from pressures. As they see it, citizen involvement often takes the form of opposition to new subjects and procedures which teachers wish to try.

Educators in the United States are in a quandary in that money for schools comes mostly from local citizens of the city or county. To secure their continual financial support it is felt that citizens must be encouraged to be interested in schools. Once aroused, citizen interest leads to discoveries that test scores in reading are lower this year over last year or that a new course in sex education is being offered to their fragile children. Lacking a system where-

Conclusions [195]

by financial support of schools comes automatically, and not trusting England's system where money and control come chiefly from the national government level, American educators try to walk a narrow line between citizen involvement and citizen interference. England's problem is not so much citizen interference as the difficulty of citizens, and teachers and local governments, having a chance to influence educational policy when the reins of power rest rather tightly in the hands of the national government. It has become clear that the national government is now the primary judge of what is important or unimportant in education.

NOTES

1. Harold Howe, "A Nation of Amateurs." School and Society, Dec. 10, 1966, p. 449.
2. Myron Lieberman, *The Future of Public Education*. Chicago: Univ. of Chicago Press, 1960, p. 75.
3. Frank Musgrove and Philip H. Taylor, *Society and the Teachers Role*. London: Routledge and Kegan Paul, 1969, p. 9.
4. W. O. Lester Smith, *Education in Great Britain*, 4th ed. London: Oxford Univ. Press, 1964, p. 9
5. Thomas H. Eliot, "Toward an Understanding of Public School Politics," pp. 163-167 in Emanuel Hurwitz and Robert Maidment, eds., *Criticism, Conflict and Change; Readings in American Education*. New York: Dodd, Mead, 1970.

INDEX

Accountability, 94, 102-103
Advisory commissions, 70-73
American Federation of Teachers, 84
Associations: Professional, 84
Association of Assistant Masters, 89, 101
Association of Education Committees, 47, 62, 100, 136, 141
Association of University Teachers, 28, 58, 60
Autonomy: for chief education officers, 129-131; for headmasters and principals, 91-92, 110-117, 128-129, 185; for higher education, 53-56, 59-60, 186; for local governments, 17-18, 23, 135-144; for schools, 92; for teachers, 50, 83-84, 90-94, 147-148, 190

"Ban the Cane," 95
"Black Papers," 168-172
Board of Governors, 121-127
Board of Managers, *see* Board of Governors
Bureaucratization: of schools, 98-99, 101-102, 111, 128
Burnham Committee, 60-62

Central Advisory Council, 70-71
Central government: powers over education, 25-37, 136-137
Centralization of power, 39-82, 191
Central government control, 22-23, 39-82
Chief Education Officer, 28, 127-131, 194
Children and Their Schools: see Plowden Report
Church schools, 28, 32, 40, 124, 126, 138, 190-191

Collective bargaining, 91, 99
Community control: of schools, 17-18, 21-22, 121-122, 138-139, 148-151, 154, 177-181, 194
Comprehensive schools, 73-79, 89-90, 113, 154, 186
Confederation for the Advancement of State Education, 77, 152, 160-166, 173, 177-178
Conservative Party, 17-18, 45, 73, 75-78, 90, 160-163
Curriculum, 46-50, 90-94

Decentralization, 50, 153, 178-179
Democracy: in schools, 96-99
Department of Education and Science, mentioned on p. 19 and included on most pages thereafter
Discipline, 95

Education Act of 1944, 26, 39-41, 70, 124
Education Committee, 100-101, 137-138, 142-143
Educational planning, 18-19, 42, 189
"Educational Priority Areas," 65-66, 176

Financing of schools, 43-46
Free schools, 95, 168

Grammar school, 73-76, 78-79, 89-90, 93, 113, 154

Headmaster, *see* head teacher
Headmaster's Conference, 50
Head teacher, 97-98, 109-119, 192-194
Higher education, 52-60
HMIs (Her Majesty's Inspectors), 28, 33-35, 47, 119, 128

[197]

Innovation, 42, 118-119, 136, 177, 193

Joint Four, 90

Labor Party, 17-18, 53, 65, 73-75, 78, 104, 144, 159-160
Liberal Party, 49
Local control of education, 16-17, 21-23, 135-145, 190-191
Local Education Authority (LEA), mentioned on p. 18 and most pages thereafter; *see* particularly 135-145

Maud Report, 18, 117, 131, 141-143
Militancy: teacher, 84-88, 101-105, 188; pupil, 119-121

National Association of Schoolmasters, 70, 86, 95, 104, 117
National Education Association, 46, 84-85
National Foundation for Educational Research, 51
National government: powers, 25-37
National planning, 18-19
National Union of Teachers, 43, 61, 65, 84-88, 90, 95, 97-105, 115-116, 121, 131, 142, 162, 192
Nursery education, 66, 174

Open classrooms, 93, 94-95, 118

Parliament, 68-69, 174, 191
Parent-teacher associations, 149, 155-157

Participation: by citizens, 147-184, 194-195; by students, 119-121; by teachers, 99-101
Plowden Report, 72, 97, 100, 114-115, 123-125, 155-158
Politics: in education, 21-22, 136
Pre-School Playgroups Association, 174
Principal, 111-113, 115, 118-119
Private schools, 17, 53, 64-65, 71, 166-168, 185
Progressive education, 91, 166-169, 172
Pupil power, 119-121

Racial factors in education, 16-17, 22, 50, 64, 130, 153, 164-165, 178-180
Research: educational, 51-52
Robbins Report, 56, 58-59, 140-141

Salaries: teachers, 60-63; professors, 60
School board, 17, 137, 139, 179
Schools Council, 48-51, 93-94
Serrano v. Priest, 46
Strikes: by teachers, 21, 62, 104-105, 115-116, 188
Student protest, 57, 67
Superintendent, 99, 127-128, 139

Teacher: centers, 49; power, 83-108; training, 42, 58-59, 192-193

Unions: teachers, 18
University Grants Committee, 28, 54-55

Voucher plan, 166-167
Violence in schools, 70, 95

"Working-to-rule," 103-104

ABOUT THE AUTHOR

GEORGE A. MALE is professor of Comparative Education and Director of the Comparative Education Center of the University of Maryland. From 1957 to 1966 he was head of the Western European unit of the Bureau of International Education, U.S. Office of Education. Prior to that he was Associate Professor of Education at the University of Vermont. He has been a visiting professor at the University of Illinois, Pennsylvania State University, Indiana University, and McGill University of Canada. He is a charter member of the European Comparative Education Society, being one of the two Americans present at the first organizational meeting. In the American Comparative and International Education Society he has served as vice president and as a member of the Board of Directors. He served also as a member of the Commission on International Education of Phi Delta Kappa. Currently he is a member of the Board of Trustees of the Inter-University International Teacher Education Council. His publications include *Education in France; Teacher Training in Belgium, Luxembourg and the Netherlands;* "Student Protest in France" in William W. Brickman and Stanley Lehrer (eds.), *Conflict and Change on the Campus;* and "Religion, Education and Morality in England," Research Paper No. 1, 1968-1969, Comparative Education Center, University of Maryland.